D0524629

The Pampered Chef®

Celebrate!
Family, Friends & Great Food

Our most treasured memories often center on a special celebration: a traditional holiday, a birthday or engagement, or a reunion with dear friends. Whatever the occasion, it is certain to become more memorable with delicious food, lovingly prepared and generously shared at the family table. And so, it is with great pleasure that we bring you *Celebrate! Family, Friends & Great Food* — a heartwarming collection of tantalizing recipes and fresh ideas to suit just about any occasion, any time of the year.

Welcome guests with an array of irresistible appetizers guaranteed to liven up any get-together. Gather loved ones around the table for a bounty of satisfying main dish and side dish recipes that combine the traditions of yesterday with the flavors of today. Leave a lasting impression on family and friends with luscious desserts from the simplest confections to the most elegant pastries, pies, and cakes.

Whether you're hosting a spectacular holiday feast or a casual backyard party, you'll be inspired by the beautifully photographed recipes, cook's tips, menu ideas, and serving suggestions that make planning and preparing for any event more enjoyable. Let our make-ahead directions, preparation and cooking time guidelines, and Pampered Chef kitchen tools help you streamline your cooking so you'll have more time to spend with family and friends. So, we warmly invite you to choose among a wealth of fabulous recipes, entertaining tips, and gift-giving ideas so that you can create your own fond memories with the special people in your life.

Celebrate!

The Pampered Chef Test Kitchens

On the cover: Step-Ahead Sweet Potato Bake (p. 51), Roast Breast of Turkey with Apple Scented Pan Gravy (p. 44), French Apple Pastry (p. 92)

Copyright ©2001 The Pampered Chef, Ltd. All rights reserved. Printed in the U.S.A.

The Pampered Chef is the premier direct-seller of high-quality kitchen tools sold through in-home Kitchen Shows. Founded in 1980 by educator and home economist Doris Christopher, and headquartered in Addison, Illinois, The Pampered Chef is committed to enhancing family life by providing quality kitchen products supported by superior service and information.

Contents

First Impressions 4

An appealing assortment of awesome, attention-getting appetizers

From dazzling to dressed-down, every celebration gets off to a great start when a variety of flavorful finger foods is available for nibbling. Appetizers set the tone for the event, and we've assembled an array of fanciful, fun, and fuss-free tidbits to get the party rolling. Our beautiful *Baked Brie with Apples & Cranberries* will delight the best-dressed crowd. *Hot Artichoke Crabmeat Dip* is a classic and always in style no matter the occasion while our fresh, innovative salsas and snacks are perfectly suited for drop-in guests. These tasty morsels are versatile, often portable, and (trust us) all are delightfully delicious.

Shrimp Wonton Cups (p. 7), Asian Sweet and Sour Meatballs (p. 9)

Center Stage 40

A marvelous menu of memorable main dishes and more

From brunch to lunch to hearty dinners, this all-inclusive chapter will help you plan your next event with ease. Many of our enticing main dish entrées are paired with sensational side dishes, making menu planning a breeze. For holiday feasting, offer a classic beef rib roast, savory turkey breast or succulent glazed ham with all the trimmings. Easy, make-ahead recipes like *Pasta Party Bowl* and *Mexican Two Bean Chicken Chili* are casual crowd-pleasers that need little more than a crisp salad and crusty bread to complete the meal. Summer picnic and patio parties call for such favorites as fresh salmon steaks, juicy pork tenderloin and zesty Italian sausages hot off the grill. Many of the recipes in this collection can be made ahead of time, which means less stress for you on the big day. Best of all, you won't lose track of the conversation, because you'll be right there to join in.

Lemon-Dill Grilled Salmon & Asparagus (p. 75)

Sweet Endings 84

A dazzling display of delightful, delectable, dream-come-true desserts

The happy commotion that accompanies many gatherings often culminates with a bit of sweet nostalgia. This chapter combines the comforting flavors of time-honored desserts with a contemporary twist along with new irresistible treats. Traditionalists will love the homey flavors of *French Apple Pastry, Harvest Honey Cake* and *Candy Cane Coffee Cake*. Variety-seekers can choose from a stunning cookie sampler suitable for all occasions to bite-size miniatures like luscious *Teatime Tartlets* and decadent *Tuxedo Brownie Cups*. For the romantic or young-at-heart, we offer *Dazzle Berry Pie, Bride-to-Be Party Cake* and spectacular *Ice Cream Pizza*. These impressive desserts will leave guests *and* the host smiling contentedly at the end of the meal – especially when they ask for seconds.

Tuxedo Brownie Cups (p. 100)

Recipe Index................125

About Our Recipes................128

Notes on Nutrition................128

Metric Conversion Chart 128

First Impressions

An appealing assortment of awesome, attention-getting appetizers

Baked Brie with Apples & Cranberries (p. 6)

Baked Brie with Apples & Cranberries

Our Small Bar Pan keeps this classy appetizer warm, allowing guests to savor every bite. (Pictured on p. 4-5)

Prep time: 15 minutes
Bake time: 12-15 minutes

Cook's Tips

Brie is a French cheese known for its soft texture and downy, white rind. When preparing Brie, leave the rind on the cheese. The entire cheese is edible, including the rind. An 8-ounce wedge of Brie can be substituted for the round.

Substitute ground cinnamon for the Korintje Cinnamon, if desired.

Golden raisins or dried cherries can be substituted for dried cranberries, if desired.

Prepared basil pesto, which is often packaged in tubs, can be found in the refrigerated fresh pasta or Italian foods section of the supermarket. Its distinctive flavor comes from fresh basil leaves, garlic, pine nuts, Parmesan cheese and olive oil.

¹/₂ cup chopped apple (¹/₂ medium)
¹/₄ cup sliced natural almonds
¹/₄ cup dried cranberries
  1 tablespoon packed brown sugar
¹/₄ teaspoon Pantry Korintje Cinnamon
  1 tablespoon butter or margarine, melted
  1 round (8 ounces) Brie cheese (about 4 inches in diameter)
     Canapé French Bread (p. 25), toasted

1. Preheat oven to 350°F. Coarsely chop apple with **Food Chopper**. Combine apple, almonds, cranberries, brown sugar and cinnamon in **Small Batter Bowl**; mix gently. Stir in butter just until ingredients are moistened.

2. Cut Brie in half horizontally using **Utility Knife**. Place one half of Brie, rind side down, on **Small Bar Pan**. Spoon half of the apple mixture onto bottom half of Brie, spreading evenly. Top with remaining half of Brie, rind side up. Spoon remaining apple mixture over top. Bake 12-15 minutes or until cheese is soft and just begins to melt. Serve with toasted *Canapé French Bread*, apple wedges or assorted crackers.

Yield: 8 servings

Nutrients per serving: Calories 150, Total Fat 11 g, Saturated Fat 6 g, Cholesterol 30 mg, Carbohydrate 7 g, Protein 7 g, Sodium 200 mg, Fiber less than 1 g
Diabetic exchanges per serving: ¹/₂ starch, 1 meat, 1 fat (¹/₂ carb)

Variation: *Baked Brie with Pesto & Mushrooms:* Using Food Chopper, chop 4 ounces mushrooms (1 cup) and ¹/₂ cup seasoned croutons. In **Small (8-in.) Sauté Pan**, cook mushrooms in 2 teaspoons olive oil 2-3 minutes over medium-high heat; remove pan from heat. Add chopped croutons and ¹/₄ cup prepared basil pesto; mix gently. Assemble and bake Brie as recipe directs. Garnish with red bell pepper strips.

Celebrate with Style

For special holiday gatherings, this elegant appetizer can be the centerpiece of a complete cheese tray. Add several other cheeses, from mild to sharp, bread sticks, crackers, apples, pears and grapes for a sophisticated party offering.

Shrimp Wonton Cups

These bite-size appetizers are packed with flavor and perfectly suited for a holiday buffet table or open house. (Pictured on p. 8)

Prep time: 25 minutes
Bake time: 13 minutes

24 square wonton wrappers

1 tablespoon butter or margarine, melted

10 ounces shelled, deveined, cooked medium shrimp, chopped

2 green onions with tops, finely chopped

1/3 cup grated carrot

4 ounces cream cheese, softened

1 garlic clove, pressed

1/2 teaspoon Worcestershire sauce

1 cup (4 ounces) shredded mozzarella cheese

1. Preheat oven to 350°F. Lightly spray **Deluxe Mini-Muffin Pan** with nonstick cooking spray. Using **Pastry Brush**, brush one side of each wonton square with melted butter. Press each wonton, buttered side up, into muffin cup. Bake 8 minutes or until edges turn light golden brown. Remove pan from oven to **Cooling Rack**.

2. Meanwhile, reserve 24 shrimp. Finely chop remaining shrimp with **Food Chopper**. Finely chop green onions with **Chef's Knife**. Grate carrot using **Deluxe Cheese Grater** fitted with coarse grating drum.

3. Combine cream cheese, garlic pressed with **Garlic Press** and Worcestershire sauce in **Classic Batter Bowl**; blend well. Stir in chopped shrimp, green onions, carrot and mozzarella cheese.

4. Using **Small Scoop**, fill each wonton cup with rounded scoop of cream cheese mixture; top with a reserved shrimp. Bake 5 minutes or until wontons are golden brown and filling is bubbly around edges.

Yield: 24 appetizers

LOW FAT Nutrients per serving (1 wonton cup): Calories 70, Total Fat 3.5 g, Saturated Fat 2 g, Cholesterol 30 mg, Carbohydrate 5 g, Protein 6 g, Sodium 110 mg, Fiber 0 g
Diabetic exchanges per serving (1 wonton cup): 1/2 starch, 1/2 fat (1/2 carb)

Cook's Tips

Wonton wrappers are paper-thin sheets of dough used to make filled wontons and egg rolls. They can be found in the produce section of most supermarkets.

Unfilled wonton cups can be prepared up to 1 week in advance. Prepare cups as directed in Step 1. Cool completely in pan. Remove and store in resealable plastic food storage bag or airtight container. Before serving, place wonton cups in muffin pan. Preheat oven to 350°F. Prepare filling and continue as recipe directs.

Celebrate with Style

For a party with Asian flair, accompany these appetizer cups with *Asian Sweet and Sour Meatballs (p. 9)*, *Summer Pizza (p. 19)* and a fruit platter with melon balls and mango chunks sprinkled with chopped fresh mint. Look for rice-paper cocktail napkins and small cocktail forks or picks at a party store or Asian market.

Asian Sweet and Sour Meatballs

East meets West when an American party favorite is infused with Asian flavor.

Prep time: 30 minutes
Bake time: 30 minutes

1/2 cup finely chopped water
   chestnuts

  1 teaspoon peeled, finely chopped
   fresh gingerroot, divided

1/3 cup thinly sliced green onions
   with tops

1 1/4 pounds lean ground turkey
   or beef

1 1/2 cups soft white bread crumbs

  3 tablespoons soy sauce

  1 garlic clove, pressed

3/4 cup plum preserves

1/4 cup chili sauce

1. Preheat oven to 400°F. Finely chop water chestnuts and gingerroot using **Food Chopper**. Slice green onions with **Chef's Knife**.

2. Combine turkey, bread crumbs, water chestnuts, 1/2 teaspoon of the gingerroot, green onions, soy sauce and garlic in **Classic Batter Bowl**; mix gently but thoroughly.

3. Using **Small Scoop**, shape meat mixture into balls; place in a single layer in **Deep Dish Baker**. Bake 15 minutes; remove from oven. Remove juices from baker using **Baster** and discard.

4. Meanwhile, combine preserves, chili sauce and remaining 1/2 teaspoon gingerroot; pour over meatballs and mix gently to coat meatballs evenly. Return to oven; continue baking 15 minutes. Stir before serving.

Yield: 10 servings (about 40 meatballs)

Nutrients per serving (4 meatballs): Calories 190, Total Fat 5 g, Saturated Fat 1.5 g, Cholesterol 45 mg, Carbohydrate 25 g, Protein 12 g, Sodium 570 mg, Fiber less than 1 g
Diabetic exchanges per serving (4 meatballs): 1 1/2 starch, 1 meat (1 1/2 carb)

Cook's Tips

To make ahead, prepare meatballs as directed. Bake 25 minutes without plum sauce. Cool and place in resealable plastic freezer bag for up to 1 month. To reheat, thaw overnight in refrigerator. Remove from bag and place in baker. Prepare plum sauce; pour over meatballs and mix gently. Bake at 400°F for 15 minutes or until heated through. Stir gently.

Gingerroot has a paper-thin, tan-colored skin that should be removed before use. Store gingerroot in a resealable plastic food storage bag in the refrigerator for up to 3 weeks or in the freezer for up to 6 months. To use frozen gingerroot, just slice off as much as you need.

Use the Food Chopper to make fresh bread crumbs. One slice of bread makes about 1/2 cup soft crumbs.

Celebrate with Style

Glazed stoneware bakers let you bake and serve with style. The glazed Deep Dish Baker is an attractive serving piece that will keep these Asian meatballs hot while the party rolls along.

Layered Athenian Cheese Spread

With holiday spirit, this molded cheese spread combines tender spinach, sweet red peppers and tangy feta and cream cheeses for all-out great flavor.

Prep time: 20 minutes
Chill time: 3 hours

2 packages (8 ounces each) cream cheese, softened

2 packages (4 ounces each) crumbled feta cheese

1 garlic clove, pressed

1 package (10 ounces) frozen chopped spinach, thawed and well drained

1 jar (7 ounces) sweet roasted red peppers, drained and patted dry

1/3 cup whole natural almonds, chopped

Canapé French Bread (p. 25), toasted

1. Combine cream cheese and feta cheese in **Classic Batter Bowl**. Press garlic over cheese mixture using **Garlic Press**; mix well. Stir in spinach.

2. Chop red peppers using **Food Chopper**. Line **Small Batter Bowl** with plastic wrap; divide cheese mixture in half. Press half of the cheese mixture into small batter bowl; top with red peppers. Spread remaining cheese mixture over red peppers. Cover; refrigerate several hours to allow flavors to blend.

3. To serve, invert onto serving plate. Remove plastic wrap. Chop almonds with food chopper; press onto top of molded cheese. Serve with toasted *Canapé French Bread (p. 25)* or assorted crackers.

Yield: 20 servings

Nutrients per serving (about 3 tablespoons): Calories 130, Total Fat 12 g, Saturated Fat 7 g, Cholesterol 35 mg, Carbohydrate 2 g, Protein 5 g, Sodium 250 mg, Fiber less than 1 g
Diabetic exchanges per serving: 1/2 meat, 1 1/2 fat

Cook's Tip

You can make this recipe early in the morning on the day of your party. The flavors will be blended even better.

Celebrate with Style

This festive cheese spread is an easy appetizer to tote along to any party setting. Just keep spread in the Small Batter Bowl, covered with the lid, while toting. Once at the party, simply unmold spread onto a serving plate, remove plastic wrap and sprinkle with chopped almonds.

Hot Artichoke Crabmeat Dip

Cozy up to the fireplace with family and friends and enjoy this restaurant-style dip at home.

Prep time: 20 minutes
Bake time: 25-30 minutes

1 package (8 ounces) cream cheese, softened
1 cup mayonnaise
1 garlic clove, pressed
1 can (14 ounces) artichoke hearts in water, drained and chopped
1 package (8 ounces) imitation crabmeat, chopped (1¹/2 cups)
³/4 cup (3 ounces) grated fresh Parmesan cheese
¹/3 cup thinly sliced green onions with tops
1 lemon
¹/8 teaspoon ground black pepper
¹/3 cup chopped red bell pepper
   Additional sliced green onions
   Baked Pita Chips (recipe follows)

1. Preheat oven to 350°F. Combine cream cheese and mayonnaise in **Classic Batter Bowl**; mix well. Press garlic into batter bowl using **Garlic Press**.

2. Using **Small Colander**, drain artichokes. Chop artichokes and crabmeat using **Food Chopper**. Grate Parmesan cheese using **Deluxe Cheese Grater**. Slice green onions with **Chef's Knife**. Zest lemon with **Lemon Zester/Scorer** to measure 1 teaspoon zest. Add artichokes, crabmeat, Parmesan cheese, green onions, lemon zest and black pepper to batter bowl; mix well.

3. Spoon mixture into **Deep Dish Baker**. Bake 25-30 minutes or until golden brown around edges. Sprinkle with red bell pepper and additional green onions. Serve with *Baked Pita Chips*.

Yield: 4 cups (16 servings)

Nutrients per serving (¹/4 cup dip): Calories 200, Total Fat 18 g, Saturated Fat 6 g, Cholesterol 30 mg, Carbohydrate 5 g, Protein 6 g, Sodium 480 mg, Fiber 1 g
Diabetic exchanges per serving (¹/4 cup dip): 1 vegetable, ¹/2 meat, 3 fat

Cook's Tips

Any style of imitation crabmeat – chunk, flake or leg – can be used in this recipe.

Dip can be made up to a day in advance. To make ahead, spoon mixture into baker, cover and refrigerate. When ready to serve, remove baker from refrigerator while preheating oven. Bake, uncovered, as recipe directs.

Baked Pita Chips

Prep time: 5 minutes   Bake time: 8-10 minutes per batch

7 whole pita bread rounds

1. Preheat oven to 400°F. Cut each pita bread in half horizontally. Cut each half into 8 triangles. Arrange in single layer on flat **Baking Stone**.

2. Bake 8-10 minutes or until lightly browned. Repeat until all chips are baked. Cool on **Cooling Rack**.

Yield: 112 chips (16 servings)

LOW FAT   Nutrients per serving (7 chips): Calories 50, Total Fat 0 g, Saturated Fat 0 g, Cholesterol 0 mg, Carbohydrate 15 g, Protein 2 g, Sodium 140 mg, Fiber less than 1 g
Diabetic exchanges per serving (7 chips): 1 starch (1 carb)

Stuffed Portobello Mushrooms

The "king" of mushrooms is crowned with Italian toppings and baked to a royal finish in our Deep Dish Baker.

Prep time: 20 minutes
Bake time: 16-18 minutes

4 medium portobello mushroom caps (3-4 inches in diameter)

1 tablespoon Italian salad dressing or olive oil

3 medium plum tomatoes, seeded and chopped (about 1 cup chopped)

2 tablespoons snipped fresh basil leaves

2 garlic cloves, pressed

3/4 cup (3 ounces) shredded Italian cheese blend

2 tablespoons seasoned dry bread crumbs

1. Preheat oven to 425°F. Brush outside only of mushroom caps with dressing using **Pastry Brush**. Place mushrooms, gill side up, in **Deep Dish Baker**.

2. Chop tomatoes using **Chef's Knife**. Snip basil with **Kitchen Shears**. Place tomatoes and basil in **Small Batter Bowl**. Press garlic into batter bowl using **Garlic Press**. Add cheese and bread crumbs; mix gently.

3. Using **Medium Scoop**, scoop mixture evenly into mushroom caps. Bake 16-18 minutes or until mushrooms are tender. Remove mushrooms to serving plate using **Mini-Serving Spatula**. To serve, cut mushrooms in half.

Yield: 8 servings

Nutrients per serving (1/2 mushroom): Calories 70, Total Fat 4 g, Saturated Fat 1.5 g, Cholesterol 5 mg, Carbohydrate 4 g, Protein 4 g, Sodium 140 mg, Fiber less than 1 g
Diabetic exchanges per serving (1/2 mushroom): 1 vegetable, 1 fat

Cook's Tips

Serving a larger crowd? This recipe can be easily doubled. To make 8 mushrooms, bake in the **Rectangular Baker***.*

Store fresh mushrooms in a paper bag in the refrigerator to extend their shelf life. Plastic-wrapped trays and airtight containers trap moisture and can cause mushrooms to spoil quickly. Use mushrooms within 2 days of purchase.

Mushrooms should not be cleaned until ready to use. To remove dirt, wipe mushrooms with a damp paper towel or soft brush, or quickly rinse under cold running water and immediately pat dry.

To easily remove the seeds from plum tomatoes, cut tomatoes in half crosswise then gently squeeze each half to release seeds.

Celebrate with Style

Delight your dinner guests with an Italian menu tonight. Follow *Stuffed Portobello Mushrooms* with a salad of mixed greens, your favorite homemade lasagna and crusty Italian bread with olive oil for dipping. Creamy *Cappuccino Mousse Trifle* (p. 120) makes an impressive finale.

Warm Olive Bruschetta

With flavors reminiscent of the sunny Mediterranean, these toasted French bread slices are spread with a savory cream cheese then topped with a robust chopped olive medley.

Prep time: 20 minutes
Bake time: 16-20 minutes

24 slices French bread, cut 1/4 inch thick

3 tablespoons olive oil

1/2 cup chopped celery

1/2 cup chopped pitted ripe olives

1/2 cup chopped pimento-stuffed green olives

2 garlic cloves, pressed

1 tablespoon Italian salad dressing

3/4 cup chive and onion cream cheese spread

Cherry tomatoes, cut into quarters (optional)

1. Preheat oven to 375°F. Place bread slices on **Large Round Stone**. Lightly brush tops of bread slices with olive oil using **Pastry Brush**. Bake 10-12 minutes or until lightly browned and crisp. Remove bread from oven and set aside.

2. Meanwhile, chop celery and olives using **Food Chopper**; place in **Small Batter Bowl**. Press garlic into batter bowl using **Garlic Press**. Add dressing; mix well.

3. Spread cream cheese evenly over toast slices using **All-Purpose Spreader.** Top with olive mixture using **Small Scoop**. Return to oven; bake 6-8 minutes or until warm. Serve bruschetta on **Round Platter**. Garnish with cherry tomatoes, if desired.

Yield: 24 appetizers

Nutrients per serving (1 appetizer): Calories 120, Total Fat 6 g, Saturated Fat 2 g, Cholesterol 5 mg, Carbohydrate 14 g, Protein 3 g, Sodium 290 mg, Fiber less than 1 g
Diabetic exchanges per serving (1 appetizer): 1 starch, 1 fat (1 carb)

Cook's Tips

Save time on the day of your party by making the olive mixture a day in advance. Just keep it refrigerated in a covered container until you're ready to use.

This recipe can be served cold, if desired. Prepare olive mixture; cover and refrigerate until ready to use. When ready to serve, spread toasted bread slices with cream cheese and top with olive mixture as recipe directs.

*The **Handy Scraper** is perfect for transferring the chopped celery and olives from the **Cutting Board** to the Small Batter Bowl.*

Four Seasons Appetizer Pizza

A Pampered Chef classic gets updated for each season and any occasion with our exclusive seasoning mixes and tasty toppers.

Prep time: 25 minutes
Bake time: 14-17 minutes
Cool time: 45 minutes
Chill time: 30 minutes

1 package (8 ounces) refrigerated crescent rolls
1 container (8 ounces) cream cheese spread
2 tablespoons mayonnaise
1 small garlic clove, pressed
  Pantry Seasoning Mix and pizza toppers for selected variation (variations follow)

1. Preheat oven to 350°F. Unroll crescent roll dough; separate into 8 triangles. On **Classic Round Stone**, arrange triangles in a circle with points in the center and wide ends toward the outside. Using **Baker's Roller**™, roll out dough to a 12-inch circle, pressing seams together to seal. Bake 14-17 minutes or until golden brown. Cool completely on **Cooling Rack**.

2. In **Small Batter Bowl**, combine cream cheese, mayonnaise, garlic pressed with **Garlic Press** and seasoning mix for selected variation. Spread evenly over crust using **Large Spreader**.

3. Add pizza toppers for selected variation. Refrigerate 30 minutes. Cut into squares with **Pizza Cutter**; serve using **Mini-Serving Spatula**.

Yield: 10 servings

Variations: *Spring Pizza:* Add 1 teaspoon **Pantry Lemon Pepper Seasoning Mix** to the cream cheese mixture. Top pizza with 4 ounces ham, cut into short, thin pieces (1 cup); 3/4 cup chopped broccoli; 1/2 cup quartered cucumber slices; 1/3 cup chopped yellow bell pepper; and 1/8 small red onion, sliced into thin wedges.

Summer Pizza: Add 1 1/2 teaspoons **Pantry Asian Seasoning Mix** and 1/2 teaspoon soy sauce to the cream cheese mixture. Top pizza with 1/2 cup chopped red bell pepper; 1/2 cup sliced snow peas; 1 small carrot, grated; 1/4 cup chopped peanuts; and 2 tablespoons snipped fresh cilantro.

Fall Pizza: Add 1 teaspoon **Pantry Italian Seasoning Mix** to the cream cheese mixture. Top pizza with 1 jar (6 ounces) marinated artichoke hearts, patted dry on paper towels and chopped; 2 ounces cotto salami, cut into short, thin strips; 1/2 cup quartered zucchini slices; 1/4 cup sliced ripe olives; and 1 plum tomato, seeded and chopped.

Winter Pizza: Add 1 teaspoon **Pantry All-Purpose Dill Mix** to the cream cheese mixture. Top pizza with 6 ounces cooked medium shrimp (1 cup). Drizzle with 1/2 cup seafood cocktail sauce. Sprinkle with 1/2 cup chopped celery; 1/3 cup sliced ripe olives; and 2 tablespoons sliced green onion.

Nutrients per serving (combined average of all variations): Calories 220, Total Fat 16 g, Saturated Fat 7 g, Cholesterol 40 mg, Carbohydrate 13 g, Protein 5 g, Sodium 410 mg, Fiber 0 g
Diabetic exchanges per serving (combined average of all variations): 1 starch, 3 fat (1 carb)

Cook's Tips

The **Rectangle Stone** can be substituted for the Classic Round Stone, if desired. Unroll crescent roll dough; do not separate. Roll out dough to within 1 inch of edges of baking stone. Bake 14-17 minutes or until golden brown. Continue as recipe directs.

When rolling out dough, sprinkle all-purpose flour onto the Baker's Roller™ to prevent sticking.

When preparing pizza toppers, use the **Food Chopper** to chop broccoli, artichoke hearts, celery and peanuts. Slice ripe olives using the **Egg Slicer Plus®**. Use the **Deluxe Cheese Grater** to grate carrot.

These pizzas are best if refrigerated no more than 2 hours before serving.

Party Salmon Puffs

Dazzle your guests when you bring out these little delights. A savory smoked salmon filling is nestled between two layers of puffy pastry.

Prep time: 30 minutes
Bake time: 15-17 minutes
Cool time: 15 minutes

Cook's Tips

Thaw puff pastry sheets at room temperature about 30 minutes before using. To cut pastry sheet into 36 equal squares, first cut sheet along fold lines to make 3 equal strips, then down the middle of each strip to create 6 strips. Cut across strips at the middle. Cut each half crosswise into thirds.

Puff pastry squares can be baked, cooled and filled up to 3 hours in advance. Store covered in the refrigerator.

To seed a cucumber using The Corer™, trim ends off cucumber and slice in half crosswise. Gently push corer through center of each half to remove seeds.

Pastry

- 1/2 package (17.3 ounces) frozen puff pastry sheets, thawed (1 sheet)
- 1 egg
- 1 tablespoon water

Filling

- 2 packages (4.5 ounces each) refrigerated, ready-to-eat, smoked salmon, chopped (2 cups)
- 1/4 cup grated carrot
- 1 lemon
- 1 small cucumber, peeled, seeded and chopped (1/2 cup)
- 1/4 cup mayonnaise
- 1/4 cup sour cream
- 2 tablespoons finely chopped onion
- 1 tablespoon snipped fresh dill weed or 1 teaspoon dried dill weed
- Sprigs of fresh dill weed (optional)

1. Preheat oven to 425°F. For pastry, unfold thawed puff pastry sheet onto lightly floured **Rectangle Stone**. Using **Pizza Cutter**, cut into 36 equal small squares. Beat egg with water in small bowl; brush over pastry using **Pastry Brush**. Pull squares apart to separate slightly. Bake 15-17 minutes or until deep golden brown. Remove from baking stone to **Cooling Rack**; cool.

2. Meanwhile, for filling, remove skin from salmon, if necessary; chop salmon with **Food Chopper**. Grate carrot using **Deluxe Cheese Grater** fitted with coarse grating drum. Zest lemon with **Lemon Zester/Scorer** to measure 1 teaspoon zest; juice with **Juicer** to measure 2 teaspoons juice. Mix salmon, carrot, zest, juice, cucumber, mayonnaise, sour cream, onion and snipped dill in **Small Batter Bowl**.

3. Use **Quikut Paring Knife** to split each pastry square crosswise in half. Using **Small Scoop**, place scoop of salmon mixture on bottom half of each square; cover with small sprig of fresh dill weed, if desired, and top half of pastry square.

Yield: 36 appetizers

Nutrients per serving (1 puff): Calories 65, Total Fat 5 g, Saturated Fat 1 g, Cholesterol 10 mg, Carbohydrate 3 g, Protein 2 g, Sodium 85 mg, Fiber 0 g
Diabetic exchanges per serving (1 puff): 1 vegetable, 1 fat

Variation: *Party Ham Puffs:* Substitute 2 cups finely chopped deli baked ham (about 10 ounces) for the smoked salmon. Continue as recipe directs.

Celebrate with Style

Party Salmon Puffs and *Fancy Deviled Eggs* (p. 22) are lovely appetizers for many elegant occasions: bridal and baby showers, Mother's Day, Easter or any sunny spring brunch or luncheon.

Fancy Deviled Eggs

This picnic classic gets a party makeover with the addition of savory flavored cream cheese and gourmet garnishes. (Pictured on p. 21)

Prep time: 20 minutes
Cook time: 30 minutes
Chill time: 30 minutes

Cook's Tips

Substitute chive and onion or salmon cream cheese spread for the garden vegetable. Gourmet spreadable cheeses in these same flavors, as well as sun-dried tomato, are delicious substitutes, too.

To easily remove shells from hard-cooked eggs, crackle shell by tapping gently all over. Roll egg between hands to loosen shell, then peel, starting at large end. Hold egg under cold running water to help ease off shell.

*To garnish deviled eggs, use fresh herbs such as parsley, cilantro or chives. Cut baby carrots into thin strips with crinkle cutter. Score small cucumber or zucchini with **Lemon Zester/Scorer**; slice and cut into quarters. Cut grape tomatoes, radishes, olives and pickles into thin slices with **Paring Knife**. Make thin cuts into tops of green onions and place in ice water to make fans. Cut bell peppers into strips or shapes.*

6 **large eggs**

1/4 **cup garden vegetable cream cheese spread**

3 **tablespoons spoonable salad dressing or mayonnaise**

Salt and ground black pepper to taste

Optional garnishes: Fresh herbs, baby carrots, small cucumber or zucchini, grape tomatoes, radishes, olives, pickles, green onions, bell peppers and small shrimp

1. Place eggs in single layer in **Small (2-qt.) Saucepan**; add cold water to cover by about 1 inch. Quickly bring water just to boiling. Remove pan from heat; cover. Let eggs stand, covered, 20 minutes. Immediately run cold water over eggs or place them in ice water until completely cooled. Remove shells.

2. Cut eggs in half lengthwise with **Crinkle Cutter**. Carefully remove yolks to **Classic Batter Bowl**. Finely chop yolks with **Pastry Blender** or mash with fork. Stir in cream cheese and salad dressing until well blended. Season to taste with salt and black pepper.

3. Place yolk mixture in **Easy Accent® Decorator** fitted with open star tip. Pipe mixture into whites. Refrigerate at least 30 minutes to allow flavors to blend. Garnish as desired.

Yield: 12 appetizers

Nutrients per serving (1 half egg): Calories 80, Total Fat 7 g, Saturated Fat 2.5 g, Cholesterol 115 mg, Carbohydrate 0 g, Protein 3 g, Sodium 85 mg, Fiber 0 g
Diabetic exchanges per serving (1 half egg): 1/2 meat, 1 fat

Roast Beef Roll-Ups

Cut these plump rolls into appetizer-size slices, or serve as a hearty picnic sandwich. Either way, stack the ingredients in thin layers for easy rolling and neat slices. (Pictured on p. 24)

Prep time: 25 minutes
Chill time: 30 minutes

1 **container (8 ounces) cream cheese spread**

3-4 **teaspoons prepared horseradish**

6 **plum tomatoes, thinly sliced**

1 **small cucumber, thinly sliced**

1 **small red onion, thinly sliced**

8 **(6-7-inch) flour tortillas**

1/2 **pound thinly sliced deli roast beef (8 slices)**

1. Combine cream cheese and horseradish in **Small Batter Bowl**; mix well. Thinly slice tomatoes, cucumber and red onion with **Ultimate Slice & Grate**.

2. For each roll, spread tortilla evenly with 2 tablespoons cream cheese mixture using **Small Spreader**. Top with 5 tomato slices, 5 cucumber slices, 3 red onion rings and 1 roast beef slice. Roll up tortilla tightly. Repeat with remaining tortillas and filling.

3. Wrap filled tortillas individually in plastic wrap. Refrigerate, seam side down, for 30 minutes. To serve, cut each roll crosswise into thirds using **Serrated Bread Knife**. Place on lettuce-lined **Chillzanne® Platter**. Serve using **Small Serving Tongs**.

Yield: 24 appetizers

Nutrients per serving (1/3 roll): Calories 80, Total Fat 4.5 g, Saturated Fat 2.5 g, Cholesterol 15 mg, Carbohydrate 6 g, Protein 4 g, Sodium 220 mg, Fiber less than 1 g
Diabetic exchanges per serving (1/3 roll): 1/2 starch, 1 fat (1/2 carb)

Variation: *Turkey Roll-Ups:* Omit horseradish. Substitute chive and onion cream cheese spread for the cream cheese and thinly sliced deli peppered turkey breast for the roast beef slices. Prepare as recipe directs.

Cook's Tips

Being able to thinly slice the vegetables with the Ultimate Slice & Grate is the key to success when making these easy appetizer roll-ups.

Tortillas can be prepared in advance. Wrap filled tortillas individually in plastic wrap and refrigerate up to 3 hours before cutting and serving.

Left whole, these tortilla roll-ups are a delicious alternative to everyday sandwiches.

Celebrate with Style

Make-ahead appetizers let the hostess enjoy the party as much as the guests. For a light supper on the patio, serve these easy roll-ups, *Bacon, Lettuce & Tomato Dip* (p. 25), *Fancy Deviled Eggs* (p. 22), a fresh fruit platter and flavored iced tea.

Bacon, Lettuce & Tomato Dip

This appetizer spin-off of the beloved BLT sandwich will be as popular as the original.

Prep time: 15 minutes
Chill time: 3 hours

1   package (8 ounces) **cream cheese,** softened

1/2 cup **ranch salad dressing**

1   medium **tomato,** seeded and diced (about 3/4 cup)

6   **bacon slices,** crisply cooked, drained and chopped

1/2 cup finely chopped **celery**

2   tablespoons finely chopped **onion**

1   teaspoon **sugar**

    Lettuce leaves

2   loaves *Canapé French Bread* (recipe follows)

1. Place cream cheese in **Classic Batter Bowl**. Gradually stir in dressing; mix well.

2. Remove seeds from tomato; dice tomato using **Utility Knife**. Reserve 1 tablespoon for garnish. Using **Food Chopper**, chop bacon, celery and onion. Add tomato, bacon, celery, onion and sugar to cream cheese mixture; mix well. Cover; refrigerate at least 3 hours to allow flavors to blend.

3. To serve, line chilled **Chillzanne®️ Mini-Bowl** with lettuce leaves. Fill with dip. Garnish with reserved tomato. Serve with toasted *Canapé French Bread*.

Yield: 20 servings (about 2 1/2 cups dip)

Nutrients per serving (2 tablespoons dip): Calories 80, Total Fat 7 g, Saturated Fat 3 g, Cholesterol 15 mg, Carbohydrate 1 g, Protein 2 g, Sodium 95 mg, Fiber 0 g
Diabetic exchanges per serving (2 tablespoons dip): 1 1/2 fat

Canapé French Bread

Prep and bake time: 1 hour, 30 minutes   Cool time: 1 hour

1   package (11 ounces) **refrigerated French bread dough**

1. Preheat oven to 375°F. Lightly spray inside of **Bread Tube** and lids with nonstick cooking spray. Place lid on bottom of bread tube; fill tube with dough. Place lid on top. Bake, upright, 50-60 minutes. Cool 10 minutes.

2. Remove bread from tube onto **Cooling Rack**. Cool completely. Cut bread into 1/4-inch slices with **Serrated Bread Knife**. Cut slices diagonally in half, if desired.

3. To toast bread slices, *preheat oven to 350°F.* Arrange slices in single layer on flat **Baking Stone**. Bake 10-12 minutes or until light golden brown. Cool.

Yield: 24 slices (1 loaf)

LOW FAT   Nutrients per serving (2 slices): Calories 60, Total Fat 1 g, Saturated Fat 0 g, Cholesterol 0 mg, Carbohydrate 10 g, Protein 2 g, Sodium 150 mg, Fiber 0 g
Diabetic exchanges per serving (2 slices): 1 starch (1 carb)

Cook's Tips

To soften cream cheese, microwave in batter bowl on HIGH 15 seconds.

To cook bacon in microwave oven, line microwave-safe dish with food-safe paper towels. Place bacon slices in single layer on paper towels; cover with paper towels. Microwave on HIGH 4-6 minutes or until bacon is crisply cooked.

The Chillzanne®️ Mini-Bowl is great for taking foods to picnics and potlucks because it keeps foods cold for hours. Place it upright in the freezer about four hours before using to allow the unique food-safe gel within the bowl's sides plenty of time to freeze.

Chicken Enchilada Ring

*The secrets to this ring's success are crushed tortilla chips and green chilies,
which lend it an authentic enchilada flavor. Olé!*

Prep time: 25 minutes
Bake time: 20-25 minutes

Cook's Tips

*For 2 cups of chopped
cooked chicken, bake,
poach or microwave about
1 pound boneless, skinless
chicken breast halves. Or
for added convenience, use
a rotisserie-cooked chicken,
available at most large
supermarkets. A 9-ounce
package frozen diced
chicken breast, thawed,
can also be used in this
recipe.*

*To make a tortilla shell to
hold the salsa and sour
cream, preheat oven to
400°F. Lightly spray
Classic Batter Bowl with
nonstick cooking spray.
Gently press one 6-7 inch
flour tortilla into bottom of
bowl to form a shell. Bake
14-16 minutes or until
edges are lightly browned.
Cool in bowl 5 minutes;
remove to cooling rack and
cool completely. To serve,
place cooled shell in center
of baked ring and fill half
with salsa and half with
sour cream. Garnish ring
with shredded lettuce, if
desired.*

2 cups coarsely chopped cooked
  chicken (about 12 ounces)
1/4 cup chopped pitted ripe olives
1 cup (4 ounces) shredded cheddar
  and Monterey Jack cheese blend
1 can (4 ounces) chopped green
  chilies, undrained
1/2 cup mayonnaise
1 tablespoon Pantry Southwestern
  Seasoning Mix
2 plum tomatoes
1 lime
2/3 cup finely crushed corn tortilla
  chips, divided
2 packages (8 ounces each)
  refrigerated crescent rolls
1 cup salsa
1 cup sour cream

1. Preheat oven to 375°F. Chop chicken
   and olives using **Food Chopper**; place in
   Classic Batter Bowl. Add cheese, green
   chilies, mayonnaise and seasoning mix.
2. Seed and chop 1 tomato. Slice lime in
   half. Using **Juicer**, juice one half of lime
   to measure 1 teaspoon juice. Reserve
   remaining lime for garnish. Add
   chopped tomato and lime juice to
   chicken mixture.
3. Reserve 2 tablespoons crushed chips;
   add remaining chips to chicken mixture
   and mix well.
4. Sprinkle reserved crushed chips over flat
   side of **Large Grooved Cutting Board**.
   Unroll crescent dough. Place dough,
   sticky side down, onto crushed chips;
   press down lightly so chips adhere to
   dough. Separate dough into triangles.
   Arrange triangles, chip side down, in a
   circle on **Classic Round Stone** with
   wide ends overlapping in the center and
   points toward outside. (There should be
   a 5-inch diameter opening in center.)
   Using **Medium Scoop**, scoop chicken
   mixture evenly onto widest end of each
   triangle. Bring points of triangles up
   over filling and tuck under wide ends of
   dough at center of ring. (Filling will not
   be completely covered.) Bake 20-25
   minutes or until golden brown.
5. For garnish, cut remaining tomato into
   8 wedges. Cut remaining half of lime
   into 4 slices; cut in half. Arrange
   between openings of ring. Cut using
   Slice 'N Serve®. Serve with salsa and
   sour cream.

Yield: 16 servings

Nutrients per serving: Calories 280, Total Fat 19 g,
Saturated Fat 6 g, Cholesterol 40 mg, Carbohydrate 16 g,
Protein 10 g, Sodium 450 mg, Fiber less than 1 g
Diabetic exchanges per serving: 1 starch, 1 meat, 2 1/2 fat (1 carb)

Family-Style Calzone

*This king-size double-crusted pizza, filled with three cheeses and pepperoni,
fits perfectly in our Rectangular Baker.*

Prep time: 30 minutes
Bake time: 20-25 minutes
Stand time: 10 minutes

  1 egg, separated
 1/2 cup chopped pitted ripe olives
  1 container (15 ounces) part-skim
     ricotta cheese
 1 1/2 cups (6 ounces) shredded
     mozzarella cheese, divided
 1/2 cup plus 2 tablespoons
     (2 1/2 ounces) grated fresh
     Parmesan cheese, divided
 1/4 cup snipped fresh parsley
  1 pouch (16 ounces) Pantry Pizza
     Crust & Roll Mix (including
     yeast packet)
  1 tablespoon Pantry Italian
     Seasoning Mix
 1 1/4 cups very warm water
     (120°F-130°F)
  4 ounces sliced pepperoni, divided

1. Preheat oven to 425°F. Separate egg
over **Small Batter Bowl** using **Egg
Separator**. Reserve egg yolk, covered,
for later use; beat egg white lightly.
Chop olives using **Food Chopper**. Add
olives, ricotta cheese, 1/2 cup mozzarella
cheese, 1/2 cup Parmesan cheese and
parsley to batter bowl; mix well.

2. In **Classic Batter Bowl**, combine pizza
crust & roll mix, yeast packet and
seasoning mix. Add warm water and stir
until mixture forms a ball.

3. Turn dough out onto well-floured
surface. With floured hands, gently
knead dough 8-10 times. Divide dough
in half. Flour both sides of dough using
Flour/Sugar Shaker; roll out one piece
of dough to a 9 x 13-inch rectangle
using **Baker's Roller**™. Place dough in
bottom of **Rectangular Baker**, shaping
to cover bottom.

4. Sprinkle 1/2 cup mozzarella cheese over
dough to within 1/2 inch of edge. Layer
half of the pepperoni over cheese.
Spread ricotta mixture evenly over
pepperoni. Top with remaining
pepperoni and mozzarella cheese.

5. Roll out remaining dough and place
over filling. Press dough all around edge
to seal with bottom crust. Beat reserved
egg yolk and brush over surface of dough
using **Pastry Brush**. Sprinkle with
remaining Parmesan cheese. Cut slits
in top crust. Bake 20-25 minutes or
until deep golden brown. Let stand
10 minutes before cutting.

Yield: 24 servings

Nutrients per serving: Calories 160, Total Fat 7 g,
Saturated Fat 4 g, Cholesterol 25 mg, Carbohydrate 15 g,
Protein 8 g, Sodium 430 mg, Fiber 0 g
Diabetic exchanges per serving: 1 starch, 1 meat (1 carb)

Cook's Tips

Use the **Pocket
Thermometer** to
accurately check the
temperature of the water
when making the dough.
Water that is too cold will
not activate the yeast while
water that is too hot will
kill the yeast.

Substitute 1 package
(16 ounces) hot roll mix
(including yeast packet) for
the Pizza Crust & Roll
Mix and Italian seasoning
for the Italian Seasoning
Mix, if desired.

To serve calzone as a main
dish, cut into large squares.

Southwestern Snack Squares

Served hot or at room temperature, guests love this innovative and delicious variation of the ever-popular layered Mexican dip.

Prep time: 20 minutes
Bake time: 20-22 minutes

- 2 tablespoons cornmeal
- 2 packages (8 ounces each) refrigerated crescent rolls
- 1 can (16 ounces) refried black beans or refried beans
- 2 tablespoons Pantry Southwestern Seasoning Mix
- 1 1/2 cups (6 ounces) shredded sharp cheddar cheese
- 2 plum tomatoes, seeded and chopped
- 2 green onions with tops, sliced
- 1/2 cup sliced pitted ripe olives
- 1/2 cup sour cream (optional)

1. Preheat oven to 375°F. Sprinkle **Stoneware Bar Pan** with cornmeal. Unroll one package of crescent rolls across one end of pan with longest sides of dough across width of pan. Repeat with remaining package of dough, filling pan. Using **Baker's Roller™**, roll dough to seal perforations and press up sides to form crust. Bake 10-12 minutes or until light golden brown.

2. In **Small Batter Bowl**, combine refried beans and seasoning mix; spread evenly over partially baked crust. Shred cheese evenly over bean mixture using **Deluxe Cheese Grater**. Continue baking 10 minutes or until cheese is melted.

3. Meanwhile, chop tomatoes and slice green onions using **Chef's Knife**. Slice olives with **Egg Slicer Plus®**. Sprinkle vegetables over cheese. Cut into squares; dollop with sour cream, if desired. Serve warm using **Mini-Serving Spatula**.

Yield: 24 appetizer squares

Nutrients per serving (1 square): Calories 120, Total Fat 7 g, Saturated Fat 2.5 g, Cholesterol 7 mg, Carbohydrate 11 g, Protein 4 g, Sodium 270 mg, Fiber 1 g
Diabetic exchanges per serving (1 square): 1 starch, 1 fat (1 carb)

Cook's Tips

Substitute 2 teaspoons chili powder for the Southwestern Seasoning Mix, if desired.

To satisfy hearty appetites, top the bean layer with 1/2 pound cooked and crumbled lean ground beef before adding the cheddar cheese. Continue as recipe directs.

Southwestern Snack Squares can also be served at room temperature. Bake crust 13-15 minutes or until dark golden brown; cool completely. Top crust as directed, but do not bake.

*Use the **Easy Accent® Decorator** to quickly add a dollop of sour cream to each appetizer square.*

Celebrate with Style

Spice up your next casual get-together with *Southwestern Snack Squares*, *Calypso Peach Salsa* and *Plantain Chips* (p. 34), prepared guacamole and salsa with tortilla chips and plenty of sparkling fruit beverages.

Barbecued Chicken Drumsticks

Slightly sweet, smoky and mild, these drumsticks are a real crowd-pleaser.

Prep time: 20 minutes
Bake time: 1 hour

3 pounds (12-14) chicken drumsticks
2 tablespoons vegetable oil
3 tablespoons Pantry Barbecue Seasoning Mix, divided
1/2 cup apple jelly
1/4 cup ketchup
1 teaspoon cider vinegar

1. Preheat oven to 375°F. Cut a 12 x 17-inch piece of **Parchment Paper** and press into bottom and up sides of **Stoneware Bar Pan**. Rinse chicken drumsticks with cold water. Pat dry with paper towels and place in pan.

2. Brush all sides of drumsticks with oil using **Pastry Brush**. Sprinkle with 2 tablespoons of the seasoning mix, rubbing lightly into skin. Bake 40 minutes.

3. Meanwhile, mix apple jelly, ketchup, remaining 1 tablespoon seasoning mix and vinegar in **Small Micro-Cooker®**. Microwave, covered, on HIGH 1 minute; mix well. Continue microwaving, covered, 30-60 seconds or until smooth when stirred.

4. Brush chicken with half of the sauce. Continue baking 10 minutes. Turn chicken with **Nylon Tongs**; brush with remaining sauce and continue baking 10 minutes. Serve drumsticks on **Oval Platter**.

Yield: 12-14 servings

Nutrients per serving (1 drumstick): Calories 190, Total Fat 8 g, Saturated Fat 2 g, Cholesterol 45 mg, Carbohydrate 14 g, Protein 14 g, Sodium 250 mg, Fiber less than 1 g
Diabetic exchanges per serving (1 drumstick): 1 starch, 1 1/2 meat (1 carb)

Variation: *Hot Barbecued Chicken Drumsticks:* Add 3-4 teaspoons Tabasco® pepper sauce to sauce mixture and brush on chicken as recipe directs.

Cook's Tips

*Use the **Kitchen Shears** to trim any excess skin from drumsticks.*

To make paper drumstick holders, cut 3 1/2-inch squares of parchment paper. Place end of baked drumstick in center of parchment square. Press paper up around drumstick and gently twist.

*For a cool change of pace, try these glazed chicken drumsticks at your next summer picnic. After baking drumsticks, cool slightly then refrigerate until well chilled. When traveling to the party, keep them cold on the **Chillzanne® Platter**.*

Calypso Peach Salsa (p. 34), Plantain Chips (p. 34), Barbecued Chicken Drumsticks

Calypso Peach Salsa

A taste of the tropics is delightful in the summer and most welcome in the middle of a long winter. (Pictured on p. 33)

1 1/2 cups coarsely chopped, peeled fresh peaches (2 medium)

1 cup coarsely chopped honeydew melon

1 medium jalapeño pepper, seeded and finely chopped

1 cup coarsely chopped fresh pineapple

1/2 cup chopped red bell pepper

2 tablespoons snipped fresh cilantro

1 lime

2 teaspoons sugar

1/4 teaspoon salt
Plantain Chips (recipe follows)
or corn tortilla chips

1. Chop peaches, melon and jalapeño pepper using **Food Chopper**. Chop pineapple and red pepper using **Utility Knife**. Juice lime using **Juicer** to measure 2 tablespoons juice.

2. Place all ingredients in **Classic Batter Bowl**; mix gently. Spoon into chilled **Chillzanne® Mini-Bow**l. Serve with *Plantain Chips* or tortilla chips.

Yield: 12 servings (3 cups)

LOW FAT Nutrients per serving (1/4 cup): Calories 30, Total Fat 0 g, Saturated Fat 0 g, Cholesterol 0 mg, Carbohydrate 7 g, Protein 0 g, Sodium 50 mg, Fiber less than 1 g
Diabetic exchanges per serving (1/4 cup): 1/2 fruit (1/2 carb)

Cook's Tips

To peel fresh peaches, bring water to a boil in **Small (2-qt.) Saucepan**. *Carefully add peaches using* **Nylon Slotted Server**. *Remove peaches after 1 minute and plunge into a bowl of cold water. Pull off skins using* **Paring Knife**.

Frozen sliced peaches, thawed, can be substituted for fresh peaches.

Wear plastic gloves when working with jalapeño peppers; juice from the peppers can cause a burning sensation on your skin.

Plantains have an appearance similar to bananas. They are a staple in many tropical countries and are used in many of the same ways potatoes are used here in North America. Plantains cannot be eaten raw at any stage. However, they can be used in a variety of dishes, depending on the stage of ripeness.

Plantain Chips

Prep time: 20 minutes   Cook time: 2-4 minutes per batch

2 green plantains, peeled and thinly sliced (about 1 pound)

5 cups vegetable oil
Salt

1. Peel and thinly slice plantains lengthwise, using **Ultimate Slice & Grate**. Cut each slice crosswise in half.

2. Heat oil in **Family (12-in.) Skillet** over medium-high heat (375°F). In batches, fry plantains about 2-4 minutes or until edges are deep golden brown. Remove carefully. Place in single layer on paper towels. Pat dry with paper towel. Season with salt to taste.

Yield: about 3 dozen chips

Nutrients per serving (about 3 chips): Calories 90, Total Fat 4.5 g, Saturated Fat .5 g, Cholesterol 0 mg, Carbohydrate 14 g, Protein less than 1 g, Sodium 0 mg, Fiber 1 g
Diabetic exchanges per serving (about 3 chips): 1 starch, 1/2 fat (1 carb)

Southern-Style Salsa

Seasoned black-eyed peas give this salsa a deliciously distinctive sweet and smoky flavor. Scoop up some with large corn chips for a tasty surprise. (Pictured on p. 36)

1/2 cup chopped green bell pepper

1/2 cup chopped red bell pepper

1 fresh jalapeño pepper, seeded and chopped

1/4 cup sliced green onions with tops

1 tablespoon snipped fresh cilantro

1 garlic clove, pressed

1 can (15 ounces) Southern-style pre-seasoned black-eyed peas, drained and rinsed

1 cup frozen whole kernel corn, thawed

1/3 cup Italian salad dressing

1/4 teaspoon hot pepper sauce

Large corn chips or tortilla chips (optional)

1. Chop bell and jalapeño peppers using **Food Chopper**. Slice green onions with **Chef's Knife**. Snip cilantro with **Kitchen Shears**. Place peppers, onions and cilantro in **Small Batter Bowl**. Press garlic into batter bowl using **Garlic Press**.

2. Add remaining ingredients; mix gently. Refrigerate 1-2 hours to allow flavors to blend. Serve with corn chips, if desired.

Yield: 3 cups (12 servings)

Nutrients per serving (1/4 cup): Calories 80, Total Fat 3.5 g, Saturated Fat 0 g, Cholesterol 0 mg, Carbohydrate 11 g, Protein 3 g, Sodium 150 mg, Fiber 2 g
Diabetic exchanges per serving (1/4 cup): 1 starch (1 carb)

Cook's Tips

Black-eyed peas are really beans, not peas. This Southern favorite gets its name from the black, eye-shaped mark on the inner curve of the tan-colored bean. They can be purchased fresh, dried or canned. Use a canned product with seasonings added to make this recipe.

*Wear plastic gloves when working with fresh jalapeño peppers. Their seeds and membranes contain oils that will irritate your skin. Use the **Quikut Paring Knife** to cut peppers in half, them remove seeds and membranes.*

Although black beans will impart a different flavor, they can be substituted for the black-eyed peas.

Celebrate with Style

When entertaining outdoors, a chilled **Chillzanne® Mini-Bowl** will keep this salsa cool on even the hottest summer nights. Use a **Bamboo Spooner** for easy serving.

Barbecue Snack Mix

Perfect for picnics or TV snacking, this sweet and spicy mix has sure-fire flavor of hickory and mesquite.

Prep time: 10 minutes
Bake time: 45 minutes
Cool time: 10 minutes

3 cups bite-size crispy corn-rice cereal

3 cups bite-size cheddar cheese crackers

2 cups oyster crackers

2 cups miniature pretzel twists

1 cup whole natural almonds (optional)

6 tablespoons butter or margarine, melted

2 tablespoons Pantry Barbecue Seasoning Mix

1 tablespoon packed brown sugar

1 tablespoon cider vinegar

1 teaspoon Worcestershire sauce

1. Preheat oven to 250°F. Combine cereal, crackers, pretzels and almonds in **Rectangular Baker**; set aside.

2. Place butter in **Small Micro-Cooker®**; microwave on HIGH 1-1½ minutes or until melted. Stir in seasoning mix, brown sugar, vinegar and Worcestershire sauce. Pour evenly over ingredients in baker. Stir gently until well coated using **Mix 'N Scraper®**.

3. Bake 45 minutes, stirring every 15 minutes. Pour out onto large sheet of **Parchment Paper** to cool. Store in airtight container at room temperature.

Yield: 9 cups (18 servings)

Nutrients per serving (½ cup): Calories 140, Total Fat 6 g, Saturated Fat 2.5 g, Cholesterol 10 mg, Carbohydrate 18 g, Protein 2 g, Sodium 350 g, Fiber 0 g
Diabetic exchanges per serving (½ cup): 1 starch, 1 fat (1 carb)

Cook's Tips

Corn or rice cereal squares can be used in this recipe, but we prefer cereal with corn on one side and rice on the other.

You can substitute 2 cups corn chips for pretzels, if you like.

For easy entertaining, make this snack mix the day before your get-together and store it in an airtight container at room temperature.

Celebrate with Style

Look for imaginative containers when serving crispy snack mixes. Use a colorful napkin to line a basket, antique crock, pottery bowl, new flowerpot or tin pail.

Honey Mustard Dip

Creamy, tangy and super simple…this dip is shy in calories while the dippers are absolutely fat free.

Prep time: 5 minutes
Chill time: 1 hour

1 cup reduced-fat sour cream
1/2 cup reduced-fat mayonnaise
1/3 cup stone-ground mustard
2 tablespoons honey
   Assorted fresh vegetable dippers and fat-free pretzels

1. In **Small Batter Bowl**, whisk together sour cream, mayonnaise, mustard and honey until well blended using **Stainless Steel Whisk**. Cover; refrigerate at least 1 hour to allow flavors to blend.

2. Arrange vegetable dippers on **Chillzanne® Platter**. Spoon dip into **Chillzanne® Platter Divider**. Serve with pretzels.

Yield: 14 servings (1 3/4 cups)

Nutrients per serving (2 tablespoons dip): Calories 70, Total Fat 4.5 g, Saturated Fat 1.5 g, Cholesterol 10 mg, Carbohydrate 4 g, Protein 1 g, Sodium 220 mg, Fiber 0 g
Diabetic exchanges per serving (2 tablespoons dip): 1 vegetable, 1 fat

Cook's Tips

Stone-ground mustard has a grainy texture from the addition of brown mustard seeds that are whole or crushed. A country-style Dijon mustard is another type of grainy mustard that tastes wonderful in this dip.

*Cut carrots into sticks and zucchini and yellow summer squash into slices with **Crinkle Cutter**. Score cucumber lengthwise with the **Lemon Zester/Scorer** then quickly cut into uniform slices using the **Ultimate Slice & Grate**.*

*Cut off root ends of radishes with **Quikut Paring Knife**. Cut out petals from sides of radishes. Place in ice water so that petals open.*

Celebrate with Style

Cover the Chillzanne® Platter with its dome lid then snap on the **Chillzanne® Platter Handle** and this snack is ready for a picnic in the park.

Center Stage

A marvelous menu of memorable main dishes and more

Herb Seasoned Beef Rib Roast (p. 42), Individual Yorkshire Puddings (p. 43), Mushroom Sauce (p. 43)

Herb Seasoned Beef Rib Roast

This stylish holiday roast is remarkably easy to prepare. The accompanying Individual Yorkshire Puddings *bake while the roast waits to be carved. A savory mushroom-shallot sauce provides the finishing touch. (Pictured on p. 40-41)*

Prep time: 20 minutes
Bake time: 2 hours,
 15 minutes to 3 hours
Stand time: 15-20
 minutes

Cook's Tips

You may want to ask the meat retailer to remove the chine bone for easier carving. Trim fat to 1/4-inch thickness.

Once meat has been removed from the oven, it will continue to cook during the standing time due to the internal residual heat. That's why it's important to remove this roast from the oven when the thermometer registers about 10°F below a desired ending temperature of 145°F for medium rare doneness or 160°F for medium doneness. Upon carving, the beef roast will be moist and tender, and not overcooked.

2 tablespoons chopped fresh thyme leaves or 2 teaspoons dried thyme leaves

4 garlic cloves, pressed

1 teaspoon coarsely ground black pepper

1/2 teaspoon salt

6-8 pound well-trimmed beef rib roast (2-4 ribs), small end

2 medium onions, sliced

1 can (14 1/2 ounces) beef broth, divided

3/4 cup water

1. Preheat oven to 350°F. Chop thyme leaves with **Food Chopper**. Combine thyme, garlic, black pepper and salt. Press evenly over surface of beef roast.

2. Slice onions into 1/4-inch-thick slices using **Ultimate Slice & Grate**. Cover bottom of **Rectangular Baker** with onion slices. Add 3/4 cup of the beef broth and water; reserve remaining broth for *Mushroom Sauce*.

3. Place roast, fat side up, on onions in baker. Insert **Digital Thermometer** so tip is centered in thickest part, not resting in fat or touching bone. Do not cover. Roast 2 hours, 15 minutes to 2 hours, 30 minutes for medium rare; 2 hours, 45 minutes to 3 hours for medium doneness.

4. Remove roast from oven when thermometer registers 135°F for medium rare; 150°F for medium. Remove roast to **Oval Carving Platter Set**; loosely tent with aluminum foil. Temperature will rise approximately 10°F during standing. (See Cook's Tips.) Let stand 15-20 minutes to allow juices to set and for easier carving.

5. Increase oven temperature to 425°F. Using **Baster**, remove meat drippings from baker; reserve for preparing *Individual Yorkshire Puddings* (p. 43). Carve roast using **Carving Set**. Serve with *Mushroom Sauce* (p. 43).

Yield: 8-10 servings

Nutrients per serving (4 ounces cooked beef): Calories 270, Total Fat 12 g, Saturated Fat 5 g, Cholesterol 90 mg, Carbohydrate 3 g, Protein 33 g, Sodium 290 mg, Fiber 0 g
Diabetic exchanges per serving: 4 meat, 1 vegetable

Individual Yorkshire Puddings

Prep time: 5 minutes   Bake time: 25 minutes

2 eggs
1 cup milk
1 cup all-purpose flour
1/2 teaspoon salt
2 tablespoons beef fat drippings (reserved from *Herb Seasoned Beef Rib Roast*)

1. Preheat oven to 425°F. In **Small Batter Bowl**, beat eggs with **Stainless Steel Whisk**; add milk, whisking until well blended. Gradually add flour and salt; whisk until smooth.

2. Spray **Stoneware Muffin Pan** cups with nonstick cooking spray. Place 1/2 teaspoon drippings in each cup. Using **Large Scoop**, fill each cup with one level scoop of batter. Bake 25 minutes or until puffed and deep golden brown. Serve immediately with *Herb Seasoned Beef Rib Roast*.

Yield: 12 puddings

LOW FAT   Nutrients per serving (1 pudding): Calories 60, Total Fat 1.5 g, Saturated Fat .5 g, Cholesterol 35 mg, Carbohydrates 9 g, Protein 3 g, Sodium 20 mg, Fiber 0 g
Diabetic exchanges per serving (1 pudding): 1/2 starch (1/2 carb)

Mushroom Sauce

Prep time: 10 minutes   Cook time: 5 minutes

8 ounces mushrooms, sliced
1/4 cup finely chopped shallots (about 2 shallots) or green onions with tops
1 teaspoon chopped fresh thyme leaves or 1/4 teaspoon dried thyme leaves
1 tablespoon cornstarch
1 cup beef broth (reserved from *Herb Seasoned Beef Rib Roast*)
2 tablespoons butter or margarine
1 tablespoon balsamic vinegar

1. Slice mushrooms with **Egg Slicer Plus®**. Using **Food Chopper**, finely chop shallots and thyme leaves. Whisk cornstarch into beef broth until completely blended using **Nylon Spiral Whisk**.

2. Melt butter in **Large (10-in.) Sauté Pan** over medium-high heat. Cook and stir mushrooms, shallots, thyme and vinegar 2 minutes. Add beef broth mixture; cook and stir until mixture comes to a boil. Boil 1 minute, stirring constantly, until thickened. Serve with *Herb Seasoned Beef Rib Roast*.

Yield: 1 3/4 cups

LOW FAT   Nutrients per serving (3 tablespoons): Calories 40, Total Fat 2.5 g, Saturated Fat 1.5 g, Cholesterol 5 mg, Carbohydrate 3 g, Protein 1 g, Sodium 140 mg, Fiber 0 g
Diabetic exchanges per serving (3 tablespoons): 1/2 vegetable, 1/2 fat

Cook's Tips

Yorkshire pudding gets its name from England's northern country of Yorkshire. Puffy and golden brown, it's most similar to a popover. It is typically made in muffin cups or a shallow baking dish.

Butter or margarine can be substituted for the beef drippings.

The batter can be made up to an hour ahead, covered and refrigerated. Stir well before filling muffin cups.

Balsamic vinegar is an Italian vinegar made from white Trebbiano grape juice. Its dark color and pungent sweetness come from aging in barrels over a period of years. You will find it among other vinegars on the supermarket shelf.

Shallots are available year round in the produce department. They resemble small, dried onions with reddish-brown skins having purple-white cloves underneath. Remove the papery skin before chopping.

Prep time: 25 minutes
Bake time: 1 hour, 50
 minutes to 2 hours,
 20 minutes
Stand time: 10 minutes

Roast Breast of Turkey with Apple Scented Pan Gravy

This moist turkey, fragrant with rosemary and herbs and served with a delicate gravy, is perfect for any special occasion.

Turkey

- 4 **medium leeks, cut into** $1/4$**-inch slices (about** $1^1/2$ **cups)**
- 2 **medium Granny Smith apples**
- 1 **bone-in turkey breast (5-6 pounds)**
- 1 **tablespoon vegetable oil**
- 2 **teaspoons Pantry Rosemary Herb Seasoning Mix, divided**

Gravy

- **Reserved pan juices**
- 3 **tablespoons butter or margarine**
- $1/4$ **cup all-purpose flour**
- 1 **can (14**$1/2$ **ounces) chicken broth**

1. Preheat oven to 350°F. Cut leeks into $1/4$-inch slices; place in bottom of **Deep Dish Baker**. Core and wedge apples using **Apple Wedger**; add to leeks.

2. Rinse turkey with cold water; pat dry. Place turkey on top of leeks and apples; brush turkey with oil using **Pastry Brush**. Sprinkle with $1^1/2$ teaspoons of the seasoning mix. Insert **Digital Thermometer** into thickest part of breast, not touching bone.

3. Bake 1 hour, 50 minutes to 2 hours, 20 minutes or until thermometer reads 170°F and juices run clear. Remove turkey breast to **Oval Carving Platter Set**; loosely tent with aluminum foil. Let stand 10 minutes before carving.

4. Meanwhile, for gravy, strain pan juices through small **Colander** into small **Colander Bowl**. Reserve pan juices; discard leeks and apples. Skim off 1 tablespoon fat into **Small (2-qt.) Saucepan**; add butter. Heat over medium heat until butter is melted; add remaining $1/2$ teaspoon seasoning mix. Stir in flour using **Nylon Spiral Whisk**. Cook over low heat, stirring constantly, until bubbly. Gradually add remaining pan juices ($1/2$ cup) and chicken broth; bring to a boil over medium heat. Boil 1 minute, stirring constantly.

5. Carve turkey into thin slices using **Carving Set**; serve with gravy.

Yield: 10-12 servings

Nutrients per serving (4 ounces turkey, $1/4$ cup gravy):
Calories 340, Total Fat 19 g, Saturated Fat 6 g,
Cholesterol 115 mg, Carbohydrate 5 g, Protein 36 g,
Sodium 420 mg, Fiber 0 g
Diabetic exchanges per serving (4 ounces turkey, $1/4$ cup gravy):
4 meat, 1 vegetable

Cook's Tips

For smaller gatherings or for those who prefer white meat only, a whole turkey breast is a smart alternative to an entire bird.

Wash leeks well to remove any sand or grit. The white and light green areas of the leek are the most tender portions. Slice the white portion along with about 1 inch of pale green portion. Do not use the dark green leaves.

Dried rosemary can be substituted for the Rosemary Herb Seasoning Mix, if desired.

Celebrate with Style

A roast turkey breast works easily into company menus any season of the year. When the air turns cool, accompany it with *Roasted Winter Vegetables* (p. 46) or *Step-Ahead Sweet Potato Bake* (p. 51) and *French Apple Pastry* (p. 92). Come warmer weather, serve *Roasted Spring Vegetables* (p. 46), fresh spinach salad and *Ultimate Banana Split Cake* (p. 119).

Roasted Winter Vegetables

Greet the season with a colorful vegetable medley, tailored for winter or spring. (Pictured on p. 45)

1 **pound beets, trimmed and scrubbed (about 6 medium)**

1 **pound parsnips, peeled (about 3 medium)**

3 **large leeks (white and light green portion only)**

1 **pound baby carrots (about 3 cups)**

3 **tablespoons olive oil**

1 **garlic clove, pressed**

1 1/2 **teaspoons Pantry Rosemary Herb Seasoning Mix**

1/4 **teaspoon salt**

1. Preheat oven to 425°F. Cut beets into quarters and parsnips into 1-inch pieces. Cut leeks in half lengthwise, then into 2-inch pieces; set aside.

2. Combine beets, parsnips, carrots, olive oil, garlic, seasoning mix and salt in large **Colander Bowl**; toss to coat using **Mix 'N Scraper®**. Spread evenly in **Stoneware Bar Pan**. Bake 25 minutes, stirring occasionally.

3. Add leeks to vegetable mixture, stirring carefully to coat with seasoned oil. Bake an additional 10-15 minutes or until vegetables are tender and golden.

Yield: 12 servings

Nutrients per serving (1/2 cup): Calories 100, Total Fat 4 g, Saturated Fat 0.5g, Cholesterol 0 mg, Carbohydrate 17 g, Protein 2 g, Sodium 140 mg, Fiber 3 g
Diabetic exchanges per serving (1/2 cup): 1 starch, 1/2 fat (1 carb)

Variation: *Roasted Spring Vegetables:*
Substitute 1 pound fresh asparagus spears, 1 large yellow or red bell pepper and 1 red onion for the beets, parsnips and leeks. Trim asparagus and cut into 2 1/2-inch pieces; set aside. Cut bell pepper into 1 1/2-inch pieces and red onion into 8 wedges. Combine bell pepper, onion, carrots, olive oil, garlic, seasoning mix and salt in large bowl. Proceed as recipe directs, adding asparagus after 25 minutes of baking time.

Cook's Tips

Vegetables can be baked up to 2 hours ahead. Let stand at room temperature. Reheat in 350°F oven for 10-15 minutes or until warm.

To clean leeks, cut in half lengthwise before washing to remove all the sand and grit. The white and light green parts of the leek are the most tender portions. Do not use dark green leaves.

Substitute 1 1/2 teaspoons dried rosemary leaves, crushed, for the Rosemary Herb Seasoning Mix, if desired.

Celebrate with Style

Although usually a side dish, roasted vegetable mixtures are nice to serve as a main course for a light lunch. The next time you have company staying for the weekend, shop the farmer's market in the morning, then serve roasted vegetables, interesting cheeses and crusty breads for lunch.

Savory Beef Brisket

This make-ahead brisket was designed with busy hosts in mind. We've updated a classic main dish with sun-dried tomatoes, onions and herbs. (Pictured on p. 48)

Prep time: 40 minutes
Bake time: 3 hours,
   30 minutes to 4 hours

1   beef brisket (5-6 pounds)

2   garlic cloves, pressed

2   teaspoons dried thyme leaves, divided

1 1/4 teaspoons dried oregano leaves, divided

1/4 teaspoon ground black pepper

2   medium onions, sliced

1/2 cup chopped sun-dried tomatoes (dry-pack)

1   can (13 3/4 ounces) beef broth, divided

   Water

2   tablespoons cornstarch

1. *Up to two days before serving*, preheat oven to 325°F. Trim excess fat from brisket and place fat side up in **Rectangular Baker**. Press garlic over brisket using **Garlic Press**. Sprinkle with 1 1/2 teaspoons thyme, 1 teaspoon oregano and pepper.

2. Slice onions using **Ultimate Slice & Grate**. Separate slices over brisket. Sprinkle tomatoes around edges of brisket. Combine 1 cup beef broth, remaining 1/2 teaspoon thyme and 1/4 teaspoon oregano. Pour over brisket and tomatoes. Cover baker tightly with aluminum foil.

3. Bake brisket 3 1/2-4 hours or until fork-tender, using **Baster** to baste brisket with pan juices after 2 hours. Remove onions and tomatoes to refrigerator container. Wrap brisket in aluminum foil. Refrigerate vegetables, brisket and pan juices separately.

4. When ready to serve, preheat oven to 350°F. Slice brisket thinly across the grain using **Carving Knife**. Arrange slices, overlapping, in baker. Top with reserved onions and tomatoes. Discard solidified fat from pan juices. Microwave juices on HIGH 1 minute to warm. Pour 1 cup juices over meat. Cover baker with aluminum foil. Bake 30 minutes, basting once, until brisket is heated.

5. Combine remaining juices, reserved broth and enough water to equal 1 3/4 cups; heat in **Small (2-qt.) Saucepan**. Mix cornstarch and 1/4 cup cold water; stir into saucepan. Bring to a boil over medium heat, stirring constantly. Boil 1 minute. Serve with brisket.

Yield: 12 servings

Nutrients per serving (4 ounces meat, 2 1/2 tablespoons each vegetables and sauce): Calories 300, Total Fat 15 g, Saturated Fat 5 g, Cholesterol 105 mg, Carbohydrate 5 g, Protein 35 g, Sodium 270 mg, Fiber less than 1 g
Diabetic exchanges per serving: 4 meat

Celebrate with Style

Some say no Festival of Lights celebration would be complete without brisket or latkes, the fried potato pancakes that symbolize the miracle of the oil. These contemporary versions of the classic dishes will appeal even to the traditionalists around your family table.

Cook's Tips

For ease in preparation, most cooks like to prepare this tender, juicy, slow-cooking cut of beef a day or two before serving. However, it can be carved and served immediately after cooking, if desired.

Omit thickening pan juices with cornstarch, if desired. Simply heat juices and spoon over beef.

When it comes to carving meat, don't be intimidated. Once the brisket is cooked, look for the grain (the direction the meat fibers are running) and then use the Carving Knife to cut across the grain to get thin, tender slices. Brisket is a very flat piece of meat, but you can get bigger slices if you cut on a slight angle from top to bottom.

Giant Potato Pancake

With convenience potatoes and the Large Sauté Pan, Hanukkah latkes can be easier and faster to make than ever before.

Prep time: 20 minutes
Cook time: 20-26 minutes

1 medium carrot, peeled
3 tablespoons chopped fresh parsley
2 tablespoons finely chopped onion
1 package (20 ounces) refrigerated shredded hash brown potatoes
3 tablespoons all-purpose flour
1/2 teaspoon salt
Dash of ground black pepper
4 tablespoons vegetable oil, divided
Sour cream or applesauce (optional)

1. Grate carrot using **Deluxe Cheese Grater** fitted with coarse grating drum; set aside. Chop parsley and onion using **Food Chopper**. In **Classic Batter Bowl**, combine potatoes, carrot, parsley and onion; mix lightly using **Mix 'N Scraper®**.

2. Combine flour, salt and black pepper. Sprinkle over potato mixture; mix lightly.

3. Heat 2 tablespoons of the oil in **Large (10-in.) Sauté Pan** over medium heat until hot (a drop of water will sizzle). Add potato mixture and press down firmly with **Nylon Turner**. Cook 9-12 minutes or until underside of potato pancake is dark golden brown and crisp. Carefully slide potato pancake onto 10-inch (or larger) dinner plate or platter. Place second dinner plate upside down over potato pancake, firmly hold plates together, and turn over so that browned side of pancake is on top.

4. Return pan to heat; add remaining 2 tablespoons oil and gently slide potato pancake, with uncooked side down, back into pan. Press firmly with turner and continue cooking 9-12 minutes or until second side is dark golden brown and crisp. Slide onto serving platter. Cut into wedges using **Slice 'N Serve®**. Serve with sour cream or applesauce, if desired.

Yield: 6 servings

Nutrients per serving: Calories 180, Total Fat 15 g, Saturated Fat 3 g, Cholesterol 0 mg, Carbohydrate 21 g, Protein 3 g, Sodium 230 mg, Fiber 2 g
Diabetic exchanges per serving: 1 starch, 1/2 fruit, 3 fat (1 1/2 carb)

Celebrate with Style

The tradition of serving potato latkes (pancakes) for Hanukkah has more to do with the oil they are fried in than the potatoes. Over twenty-one centuries ago, when a Jewish group found they had only enough oil to light the temple's menorah for one day, the oil miraculously lasted for eight full days and nights.

Cook's Tips

Use fresh, crisp, curly-leaf parsley. Rinse under cold water and pat dry on paper towels before chopping with the food chopper. If using fresh Italian or flat-leaf parsley, snip leaves with the **Kitchen Shears***.*

The gently sloping sides of the Sauté Pan make it easy to slide the potato pancake out of the pan.

Step-Ahead Sweet Potato Bake

Dinner will be served on schedule when you do most of the preparation for this lovely harvest side dish the day before.

Prep time: 30 minutes
Bake time: 30-35 minutes

6 medium sweet potatoes
  (3 pounds)
1/2 cup packed brown sugar
3 tablespoons butter or margarine
1 teaspoon Pantry Cinnamon Plus™
  Spice Blend
1/4 teaspoon salt
1 orange
2 medium Granny Smith apples
1/2 cup fresh cranberries (optional)

1. *Up to a day in advance*, place potatoes in **Dutch (6-qt.) Oven**; add enough water to cover potatoes. Bring to a boil; cover. Cook 20-25 minutes or just until fork-tender. Drain; cool. Peel; cut crosswise into 1-inch-thick slices using **Crinkle Cutter**. Cut large slices in half. Place in **Square Baker**; cover with plastic wrap and refrigerate.

2. Place brown sugar, butter, spice blend and salt in **Large Micro-Cooker®**. Zest orange to measure 1 teaspoon zest using **Lemon Zester/Scorer**. Juice orange to measure 2 tablespoons juice using **Juicer**. Add zest and juice to micro-cooker. Microwave, covered, on HIGH 1 minute. Stir; cover and refrigerate.

3. *When ready to serve*, preheat oven to 375°F. Microwave sweet potatoes in baker on MEDIUM (50%) 5 minutes; set aside. Microwave sugar mixture on HIGH 1 minute or until blended when stirred.

4. Cut apples into wedges with **Apple Wedger**. Stir into sugar mixture. Microwave, covered, 3 minutes. Pour over sweet potatoes.

5. Bake 15 minutes. Sprinkle with cranberries, if desired. Baste sweet potatoes and apples with sugar mixture using **Baster**. Continue baking 15-20 minutes or until heated. Baste before serving.

Yield: 8 servings

Nutrients per serving: Calories 200, Total Fat 4.5 g, Saturated Fat 2.5 g, Cholesterol 10 mg, Carbohydrate 39 g, Protein 2 g, Sodium 130 mg, Fiber 3 g
Diabetic exchanges per serving: 1 starch, 1 1/2 fruit, 1/2 fat (2 1/2 carb)

Celebrate with Style

Add warmth and charm to your harvest table with a simple homemade centerpiece. Use **The Corer™** to core several large shiny apples. Place a tall, thin candle in the center of each apple then complete the arrangement with autumn leaves, flowers, gourds and bittersweet.

Cook's Tips

If you prefer not to make this sweet potato bake ahead, you don't need to refrigerate the sweet potatoes or sugar mixture, and you can omit Step 3.

*When basting sweet potatoes, remove baker to **Cooling Rack**. This way the oven will lose less heat. You may want to tip the baker slightly so that the sugar mixture pools in one area, making it easier to baste the potatoes. When it comes time for cleanup, the specially designed cleaning brush that comes with the baster makes washing it a breeze.*

Twice-Baked Potato Cups

Fabulous, no-fuss dinners are possible with make-ahead sides like this. See our Cook's Tips on how to make these delicious potatoes up to two weeks before your dinner party.

Prep time: 35 minutes
Bake time: 1 hour, 35
  minutes to 1 hour,
  40 minutes

Cook's Tips

*To make ahead up to
1 day in advance, assemble
potato cups in muffin pan,
cover and refrigerate.
When ready to serve,
remove pan from
refrigerator. Preheat oven
to 400°F. Bake,
uncovered, as recipe
directs.*

*To make ahead and freeze,
place assembled potato cups
in freezer container; freeze
up to 2 weeks. When ready
to serve, remove from
freezer and thaw in
refrigerator overnight.
Preheat oven to 400°F.
Place potato cups in muffin
pan and bake as recipe
directs.*

*Using the Easy Accent®
Decorator to pipe potato
mixture on top of cups
gives this side dish an
elegant finish that's actually
fun and easy to do.*

  6 **medium baking potatoes
      (about 8 ounces each)**
      Vegetable oil
 1/2 **cup (2 ounces) grated fresh
      Parmesan or cheddar cheese**
 1/2 **cup sour cream**
 1/2 **cup milk, heated**
  3 **green onions with tops, chopped**
 1/4 **teaspoon salt**
 1/4 **teaspoon ground back pepper**
      **Optional garnishes: sliced green
      onion tops, crisply cooked
      crumbled bacon, grated fresh
      Parmesan cheese or shredded
      cheddar cheese**

1. Preheat oven to 400°F. Scrub potatoes; brush lightly with oil using **Pastry Brush**. Pierce potatoes several times; place in **Deep Dish Baker**. Bake 1 hour 10 minutes or until fork-tender. Remove from baker to **Cooling Rack**; cool 10-15 minutes or until cool enough to handle. Meanwhile, grate cheese with **Deluxe Cheese Grater**; set aside.

2. Slice each potato crosswise in half. Carefully scoop out pulp from each potato half into **Classic Batter Bowl**, leaving a 1/4-inch-thick shell. Cut a thin slice off bottom of each potato cup; place potato cups in **Stoneware Muffin Pan**.

3. Mash potato pulp with **Nylon Masher**. Add sour cream; continue to mash until no lumps remain. Gradually beat in milk. Stir in green onions, cheese, salt and black pepper; mix well.

4. Fill **Easy Accent® Decorator** fitted with open star tip with potato mixture; set aside. Using **Large Scoop**, fill each potato cup with remaining potato mixture. Pipe reserved potato mixture over top of each potato. Bake 25-30 minutes or until heated through and golden brown. Garnish as desired.

Yield: 12 servings

LOW FAT   Nutrients per serving (1 potato cup):
           Calories 110, Total Fat 3 g, Saturated Fat 2.5 g,
Cholesterol 10 mg, Carbohydrate 17 g, Protein 4 g,
Sodium 140 mg, Fiber 2 g
Diabetic exchanges per serving (1 potato cup): 1 starch,
1/2 fat (1 carb)

Seafood Chowder

This elegant chowder is garnished with snipped parsley for a fresh finish.

Prep time: 35 minutes
Cook time: 30 minutes

4-5 medium red potatoes, cut into 1-inch cubes (about 1 pound)

1 cup chopped onion

1 cup sliced carrots

1 cup sliced celery

1 cup diced red bell pepper

2 cans ($6^1/2$ ounces each) minced clams, drained, reserving clam juice

1 tablespoon butter or margarine

2 cans ($14^1/2$ ounces each) chicken broth

$1/2$ teaspoon salt

$1/4$ teaspoon ground black pepper

$3/4$ cup all-purpose flour

2 cups half-and-half (light cream)

1 pound fresh bay scallops

1 pound frozen, cooked medium shrimp, thawed, rinsed and tails removed

Snipped fresh parsley

1. Cut potatoes into 1-inch cubes to measure 3 cups. Chop onion using **Food Chopper**. Slice carrots and celery and dice bell pepper with **Chef's Knife**.

2. Using small **Colander**, drain clams reserving clam juice. If clam juice does not measure 1 cup, add enough water to equal 1 cup.

3. Melt butter in **Dutch (6-qt.) Oven** over medium heat. Add onion; cook 3 minutes or until onion is tender. Add potatoes, carrots, celery, bell pepper, reserved clam juice, chicken broth, salt and black pepper. Bring to a boil; cover. Reduce heat and simmer 3 minutes or until potatoes are tender.

4. Meanwhile, place flour in **Small Batter Bowl**. Using **Nylon Spiral Whisk**, gradually whisk half-and-half into flour; whisk until smooth.

5. Add clams, scallops and shrimp to chowder; gradually whisk in flour mixture. Return to a boil; cook 2 minutes or until thickened, stirring constantly. Cover until ready to serve. Ladle soup into bowls using **Nylon Ladle**. Sprinkle with parsley.

Yield: 12 servings (15 cups)

Nutrients per serving (about $1^1/4$ cups): Calories 250, Total Fat 8 g, Saturated Fat 3.5 g, Cholesterol 120 mg, Carbohydrate 19 g, Protein 24 g, Sodium 620 mg, Fiber 2 g
Diabetic exchanges per serving (about $1^1/4$ cups): 1 starch, 2 meat (1 carb)

Cook's Tips

This chowder can be made 1-2 days in advance. When ready to serve, heat covered over medium-low heat until hot, stirring occasionally. Do not boil.

Bay scallops are light pink or tan and about $1/2$ inch in diameter. Sea scallops are larger, about $1^1/2$ inches in diameter. If only sea scallops are available, cut each scallop in half or in quarters before adding to the chowder. Use fresh scallops within 1 or 2 days after purchasing. Scallops can be frozen.

Celebrate with Style

Let this delicious Seafood Chowder take center stage at your special New Year's Eve dinner. Start with *Layered Athenian Cheese Spread* (p. 10) and *Stuffed Portobello Mushrooms* (p. 15). Serve a salad of mixed gourmet greens tossed with a vinaigrette dressing and add crisp bread sticks. When guests think they can't eat one more delight, tempt them with bite-size *Tuxedo Brownie Cups* (p. 100) and a tray of *All-Occasion Cookies* (p. 86).

Individual Beef Wellingtons

These pastry-enrobed beef filets are perfect for a romantic dinner for two.

1/2 package (17.3 ounces) frozen puff
    pastry sheets (1 sheet)
  2 beef tenderloin steaks, cut 1 inch
    thick (5-6 ounces each)

Vegetable Filling

1/2 cup thin carrot sticks
1/2 cup thin red bell pepper strips
1/2 cup thin zucchini sticks
  1 teaspoon olive oil
  1 garlic clove, pressed
1/8 teaspoon salt
    Dash of ground black pepper
1/2 cup (2 ounces) shredded Italian
    cheese blend

Garlic-Basil Spread

1/2 teaspoon olive oil
  1 garlic clove, pressed
  1 tablespoon snipped fresh basil
1/4 teaspoon salt
1/8 teaspoon ground black pepper

1. *Two to four hours before serving,* line **Small Bar Pan** with **Parchment Paper**. Thaw puff pastry at room temperature. Trim any fat from steaks.

2. For vegetable filling, cut vegetables into thin pieces, 2 inches long. Heat oil in **Large (10-in.) Sauté Pan** over medium heat. Add vegetables and garlic pressed with **Garlic Press**; cook and stir 5 minutes. Sprinkle with salt and black pepper. Remove to **Small Batter Bowl**; cool. Stir in cheese.

3. For garlic-basil spread, heat 1/2 teaspoon oil over medium-low heat in same pan. Press garlic into oil and cook just until softened, about 1 minute. Add garlic with oil to basil, salt and black pepper.

4. To assemble Wellingtons, gently unfold pastry. Cut along one fold line; set aside strip of pastry (1/3 of sheet). Cut remaining pastry crosswise in half to form two rectangles. Spoon half of the vegetable filling onto center of each rectangle. Spread one side of each steak with garlic-basil spread. Place steaks on vegetables, garlic-basil side down. Bring pastry corners up over steaks (most of the meat surface is not covered). Gently press pastry against sides of steaks; turn over and place steaks, pastry side up, on bar pan. Cut designs from reserved pastry; arrange over tops. Cover; refrigerate 2-4 hours.

5. When ready to serve, preheat oven to 425°F. Insert probe of **Digital Thermometer** into center of 1 Wellington. Bake 26-30 minutes or until 130°F for medium rare; 140°F for medium. Remove Wellingtons from bar pan. Let stand 5 minutes before serving. (Temperatures will rise 15°F-20°F during standing time to reach final temperatures of 145°F for medium rare; 160°F for medium doneness.)

Yield: 2 servings

Nutrients per serving: Calories 830, Total Fat 51 g, Saturated Fat 17 g, Cholesterol 165 mg, Carbohydrate 40 g, Protein 49 g, Sodium 1215 mg, Dietary Fiber 4 g
Diabetic exchanges per serving: 3 starch, 6 meat, 3 fat (3 carb)

Prep time: 50 minutes
Make-ahead chill time:
  2-4 hours
Bake time: 26-30 minutes
Stand time: 5 minutes

Cook's Tips

This recipe can be doubled and baked on the **Stoneware Bar Pan**.

Wellingtons should be removed from the oven before they reach the desired serving temperature because hot steam trapped by the pastry covering continues to cook the steaks during their short standing time.

Beef tenderloin steak is a boneless, very tender steak that is also called filet or filet mignon. For this special-occasion entrée, we recommend purchasing steaks with a quality grade of Choice. Steaks graded Select are usually less expensive, but may not be as juicy or flavorful.

To give puff pastry a shiny appearance, beat 1 egg with 1 tablespoon cold water and brush over pastry just before baking Wellingtons.

Tangy Mustard Glazed Ham

Our classic spring ham becomes a stunning centerpiece for an Easter celebration.

Prep time: 15 minutes
Bake time: 1 hour,
  50 minutes to 2 hours
Stand time: 15-20
  minutes

Cook's Tips

Be sure to read the label on the ham; some are fully cooked, some partially cooked. Since meat continues to cook after it is removed from the oven, remove ham from the oven when the thermometer registers 5°F lower than the desired end temperature. The desired temperatures for doneness are 145°F for a fully cooked ham, and 160°F for a partially cooked ham.

If using a spiral-sliced ham, do not cut diamond pattern in fat layer. Insert cloves at 1-inch intervals. Follow cooking instructions as recipe directs.

Leftover cooked ham should be wrapped and refrigerated promptly; store up to 5 days. Leftover ham can be used to prepare Ham Florentine Wreath (p. 62).

 1 **fully or partially cooked smoked bone-in ham (6-8 pounds), butt portion, see Cook's Tips**
40 **whole cloves**
1$1/2$ **cups packed brown sugar**
$1/3$ **cup stone ground mustard**
 2 **tablespoons cider vinegar**

1. Preheat oven to 325°F. Create a diamond pattern by cutting parallel lines, about 1 inch apart and $1/4$ inch deep, across the ham into the fat. Repeat, cutting at a right angle to the existing lines. Insert one whole clove in center of each diamond. Place ham in **Deep Dish Baker**, fat side up. Cover with **Stoneware Baking Bowl**. Bake 1 hour, 30 minutes.

2. Meanwhile, combine brown sugar, mustard and vinegar in **Small Batter Bowl**; mix well. Set aside $1/2$ cup brown sugar mixture to glaze ham; reserve remaining mixture for sauce.

3. Using **Oven Mitts**, pull out oven rack and carefully remove baking bowl from baker, lifting away from you. Carefully remove ham from oven (juice will have collected in bottom of baker) to **Cooling Rack**. Using **Baster**, remove pan juices, leaving some covering bottom of baker. Reserve 3 tablespoons juices; discard remaining. Using **Pastry Brush**, carefully brush $1/2$ cup glaze over ham.

4. Insert **Digital Thermometer** so tip is centered in thickest part, not resting in fat or bone. Do not cover. Return to oven and bake, uncovered, 20-30 minutes or until thermometer registers 140°F (for fully cooked ham) or 155°F (for partially cooked ham). (Temperature will rise approximately 5°F-10°F during standing.) Cover loosely with aluminum foil and let stand 15-20 minutes for easier carving.

5. Heat reserved sugar mixture with reserved juices over low heat, stirring constantly with **Nylon Spiral Whisk**. Remove cloves from ham. Transfer ham to **Oval Carving Platter Set**; slice with **Carving Set**. Serve with sauce.

Yield: 12 servings

Nutrients per serving (4 ounces ham, about 1 tablespoon sauce): Calories 340, Total Fat 17 g, Saturated Fat 5 g, Cholesterol 50 mg, Carbohydrate 31 g, Protein 15 g, Sodium 1670 mg, Fiber less than 1 g
Diabetic exchanges per serving (4 ounces ham, about 1 tablespoon sauce): 2 starch, 1$1/2$ meat, 1$1/2$ fat (2 carb)

Celebrate with Style

Twice-Baked Potato Cups (p. 52) and *Festive Scalloped Corn* (p. 61) are tasteful accompaniments to serve with this beautifully glazed ham. For dessert, enjoy *Creamy Lemon Supreme* (p. 109).

Festive Scalloped Corn

This fast-to-fix side dish promises the comforts of home and looks better than ever in our glazed Oval Baker.

Prep time: 15 minutes
Bake time: 35-40 minutes

1/3 cup chopped green onions
     with tops

3   eggs

1   can (14.75 ounces) cream-style
     corn, undrained

1   can (11 ounces) whole kernel
     corn with red and green bell
     peppers, drained

1   package (8 1/2 ounces) corn
     muffin mix

1   cup reduced-fat sour cream

2   tablespoons butter or margarine,
     melted

1/8 teaspoon ground red pepper

1. Preheat oven to 375°F. Spray **Oval Baker** with nonstick cooking spray. Chop onions using **Food Chopper**.

2. In **Classic Batter Bowl**, whisk eggs with **Stainless Steel Whisk**. Add green onions and remaining ingredients; mix until well blended using **Mix 'N Scraper®**.

3. Pour mixture into baker. Bake 35-40 minutes or until edges are golden brown.

Yield: 10 servings

Nutrients per serving: Calories 230, Total Fat 9 g, Saturated Fat 4.5 g, Cholesterol 80 mg, Carbohydrate 21 g, Protein 6 g, Sodium 290 mg, Fiber 2 g
Diabetic exchanges per serving: 1 1/2 starch, 1 fat (1 1/2 carb)

Celebrate with Style

The popularity of corn guarantees this side dish will be a welcome addition to any Easter, Thanksgiving or Christmas holiday meal, as well as an informal potluck, church supper or dinner with a Mexican theme.

Cook's Tips

Wash green onions and pat dry with paper towels before chopping.

*The small **Colander** is the perfect size for draining corn and other canned vegetables and fruits. It comes in a handy **4-Piece Colander & Bowl Set**.*

Ham Florentine Wreath

This beautifully woven, savory pastry is perfectly suited for
a casual buffet-style lunch or brunch.

2 **packages (8 ounces each) refrigerated crescent rolls**

1 **package (10 ounces) frozen chopped spinach, thawed and well drained**

1¹/₂ **cups (8 ounces) diced cooked ham**

¹/₄ **cup green onions with tops, thinly sliced**

1¹/₄ **cups (5 ounces) shredded Swiss cheese, divided**

¹/₄ **cup mayonnaise**

¹/₄ **teaspoon coarsely ground black pepper**

2 **plum tomatoes, sliced**

1 **egg white, lightly beaten**

¹/₄ **cup sliced natural almonds, chopped**

1. Preheat oven to 375°F. Unroll crescent dough; separate into 16 triangles. With wide ends of triangles toward the center, arrange 8 triangles in a circle on **Large Round Stone**. Corners of wide ends will touch and points will extend 1 inch beyond edge of baking stone. Arrange remaining 8 triangles in center, matching wide ends. Seal seams using **Baker's Roller™**. (Points will overlap in center; do not seal.)

2. For filling, combine spinach, ham and green onions in **Classic Batter Bowl**. Shred cheese using **Deluxe Cheese Grater**. Add 1 cup of the cheese, mayonnaise and black pepper to ham mixture; mix well. Using **Large Scoop**, scoop filling over seams of dough, forming a circle.

3. Arrange tomatoes in an overlapping circular pattern over filling; top with remaining cheese. Beginning in center, lift one dough triangle across mixture. Continue alternating with outer triangles, slightly overlapping to form wreath. Tuck last end under first.

4. Brush egg white over dough using **Pastry Brush**. Coarsely chop almonds using **Food Chopper**; sprinkle over wreath. Bake 25-30 minutes or until golden brown. Cut and serve using **Slice 'N Serve®**.

Yield: 10 servings

Nutrients per serving: Calories 310, Total Fat 21 g, Saturated Fat 6 g, Cholesterol 30 mg, Carbohydrate 19 g, Protein 13 g, Sodium 700 mg, Fiber 2 g
Diabetic exchanges per serving: 1 starch, 2 meat, 2 fat (1 carb)

Cook's Tips

The filling can be prepared several hours in advance. Cover and refrigerate until ready to use.

It's best not to take the crescent roll dough out of the refrigerator until just before you need it. Once the dough is warm, it becomes soft and sometimes sticky, making it difficult to work with.

Celebrate with Style

Present this lovely wreath on our glazed **Round Platter** accompanied by a fresh fruit salad, warm muffins and fresh brewed coffee.

Lemony Chicken Popover Puff

This savory popover puff features a fresh, colorful filling flavored with dill. This one-dish wonder is sure to be a hit at your next brunch or casual dinner.

Prep time: 25 minutes
Cook time: 30-35 minutes

Popover Puff

- 3 tablespoons butter or margarine, melted, divided
- 1 cup milk
- 6 eggs
- 1 cup all-purpose flour
- 1/2 teaspoon salt

Chicken & Vegetable Filling

- 2 medium carrots, peeled
- 1 cup sugar snap peas, cut in half
- 1/2 cup chopped onion
- 1 tablespoon butter or margarine
- 1 lemon
- 1 can (10 1/2 ounces) condensed cream of chicken soup
- 2 cups diced cooked chicken (12 ounces)
- 1 cup diced red bell pepper
- 1 1/2 teaspoons Pantry All-Purpose Dill Mix
- 1/2 cup (2 ounces) shredded cheddar cheese

1. Preheat oven to 450°F. For popover puff, measure 1 tablespoon of the butter into **Deep Dish Baker**; brush over bottom only. In **Classic Batter Bowl**, combine milk, eggs and remaining butter using **Stainless Steel Whisk**. In **Small Batter Bowl**, stir together flour and salt. Add flour mixture to egg mixture; whisk 1 minute or until smooth. Pour batter into baker. Bake 20 minutes. *Reduce oven temperature to 350°F; continue baking 10-15 minutes or until puffed and golden brown.*

2. Meanwhile, prepare chicken and vegetable filling. Using **Crinkle Cutter**, cut carrots in half lengthwise then crosswise into 1/2-inch slices for a total of 1 cup. Chop onion using **Food Chopper**. Place carrots, snap peas, onion and butter in **Small Micro-Cooker®**. Microwave, covered, on HIGH 2-3 minutes or until vegetables are crisp-tender; set aside.

3. Juice lemon using **Juicer** to measure 2 tablespoons juice. In clean Classic Batter Bowl, combine lemon juice, soup, chicken, bell pepper and dill mix; mix well. Microwave on HIGH 4-5 minutes or until hot, stirring once. Add cheese and half of the vegetable mixture into filling; mix gently.

4. Remove puff from oven to **Cooling Rack**; let stand 3 minutes or until puff begins to fall. If necessary, cut around sides of puff to loosen from baker. Spoon filling into puff; arrange remaining vegetable mixture around edges. Slice and serve using **Slice 'N Serve®**.

Yield: 8 servings

Nutrients per serving: Calories 360, Total Fat 19 g, Saturated Fat 8 g, Cholesterol 220 mg, Carbohydrate 22 g, Protein 23 g, Sodium 650 mg, Fiber 2 g
Diabetic exchanges per serving: 1 1/2 starch, 3 meat (1 1/2 carb)

Cook's Tips

Fresh broccoli florets can be substituted for the sugar snap peas.

Dried dill weed can be substituted for the All-Purpose Dill Mix, if desired.

This oven-baked popover gets its puffiness from the steam produced as the batter bakes. To create a popover puff with optimum volume, whisk the batter for 1 minute before pouring it into the baker.

Party Pasta Bowl

*This hearty casserole makes enough for a hungry crowd. Don't worry,
though – there won't be any leftovers to put away!*

Prep time: 35 minutes
Bake time: 1 hour,
  10 minutes

1 package (16 ounces) uncooked
  mostaccioli or ziti

1 cup chopped onion

1 pound lean (90%) ground beef

3 garlic cloves, pressed

2 teaspoons Pantry Italian
  Seasoning Mix

1 jar (48 ounces) spaghetti sauce

1 can (14.5 ounces) diced
  tomatoes, undrained

1 egg

1 container (15 ounces) part-skim
  ricotta cheese

2 cups (8 ounces) shredded
  mozzarella cheese, divided

1/4 cup snipped fresh parsley

1/4 teaspoon ground black pepper

1/2 cup (2 ounces) grated fresh
  Parmesan cheese, divided

Additional snipped fresh parsley

1. Preheat oven to 350°F. Cook pasta
according to package directions in
Dutch (6-qt.) Oven; drain.

2. Meanwhile, chop onion using **Food
Chopper**. Place onion, ground beef and
garlic pressed with **Garlic Press** in
Family (12-in.) Skillet. Cook and stir
over medium heat 8-10 minutes or until
beef is no longer pink. Remove from
heat; drain. Sprinkle with seasoning
mix. Stir in sauce and tomatoes.

3. In **Small Batter Bowl**, lightly beat egg
with **Stainless Steel Whisk**. Add ricotta
cheese, 1 cup of the mozzarella cheese,
parsley and black pepper. Grate
Parmesan cheese using **Deluxe Cheese
Grater**; set aside 1/4 cup. Stir remaining
Parmesan cheese into ricotta mixture.

4. To assemble casserole, place cooked
pasta in **Stoneware Baking Bowl**. Add
6 cups of the meat sauce; mix well.
Spread ricotta mixture evenly over
pasta. Top with remaining meat sauce.
Bake 1 hour. Top with remaining
mozzarella and Parmesan cheeses.
Continue baking 10 minutes or until
bubbly. Garnish with additional parsley.

Yield: 12 servings

Nutrients per serving: Calories 410, Total Fat 14 g,
Saturated Fat 7 g, Cholesterol 55 mg, Carbohydrate 42 g,
Protein 27 g, Sodium 800 mg, Fiber 4 g
Diabetic exchanges per serving: 2 1/2 starch, 3 meat (2 1/2 carb)

Cook's Tips

*To snip fresh parsley, rinse
parsley with cold water and
pat dry with paper towels.
Place in a small, deep bowl
and snip with the **Kitchen
Shears**.*

*The Deluxe Cheese Grater
comes with a fine grating
drum good for grating
Parmesan and other hard
cheeses and a coarse
grating drum good for firm
cheeses such as cheddar,
Monterey Jack and Colby.*

*To prepare this dish ahead
of time, assemble casserole
2-3 hours in advance,
cover and refrigerate.
When ready to serve, let
stand at room temperature
about 20 minutes then
bake, uncovered, as recipe
directs.*

Celebrate with Style

Keep your party relaxed and easy. Empty packaged salad greens into a big serving bowl then
arrange vegetable toppers on the **Chillzanne® Platter** fitted with the **Divider**. Let guests
create their own salads and offer baskets of crusty French bread. Offer bakery brownies,
ice cream, dessert toppings and candy sprinkles for build-your-own brownie sundaes.

Mexican Two Bean Chicken Chili

This chili, made with prepared salsa and a few pantry ingredients, comes together in no time so you can relax before the big game.

Prep time: 20 minutes
Cook time: 30 minutes

1 medium zucchini, coarsely chopped (about 1¼ cups)

1 can (15 ounces) black beans, drained and rinsed

1 can (15 ounces) pinto beans, drained and rinsed

1 can (8¾ ounces) whole kernel corn, drained

2 cans (14½ ounces each) chicken broth

1 jar (16 ounces) thick and chunky mild salsa

1 can (8 ounces) tomato sauce

3 cups shredded cooked chicken

1 garlic clove, pressed

1½-2 tablespoons chili powder

1 teaspoon ground cumin

Optional toppings: shredded cheese, sour cream, crushed corn or tortilla chips, sliced green onions and fresh cilantro leaves

1. Chop zucchini using **Food Chopper**. Drain and rinse beans in **Small Colander**. Drain corn.

2. Combine chicken broth, salsa and tomato sauce in **Professional (4-qt.) Casserole**. Add zucchini, beans, corn, chicken, garlic pressed with **Garlic Press**, chili powder and cumin.

3. Bring to a boil; reduce heat and simmer 30 minutes.

4. Ladle chili into soup bowls using **Nylon Ladle**. Top with desired toppings.

Yield: 6 servings (10 cups)

Nutrients per serving (1⅔ cups): Calories 310, Total Fat 9 g, Saturated Fat 2 g, Cholesterol 65 mg, Carbohydrate 29 g, Protein 29 g, Sodium 1820 mg, Fiber 8 g

Diabetic exchanges per serving (1⅔ cups): 1½ starch, 2½ meat (1½ carb)

Cook's Tips

*Shredding chicken is easy using the **Hold 'N Slice**™. The strong, stainless steel prongs will separate cooked chicken meat into thin long strands.*

In a hurry? A purchased, cooked rotisserie chicken from the supermarket deli can be used.

For chili with a little more heat, substitute medium salsa for the mild salsa.

*This recipe can easily be doubled and prepared in the **Professional (8-qt.) Stockpot**. This recipe also reheats well so you can make it ahead, if you like.*

Celebrate with Style

You'll find many casual occasions to serve this hearty Mexican chili. Always provide a selection of toppers, then let guests ladle out their soup and top it to their own liking. Freshly baked cornbread, cornbread sticks and soft flour or corn tortillas are also nice accompaniments.

Chicken Lasagna Alfredo

Guests will enjoy the balance of flavors in this creamy layered pasta dish. You'll enjoy a leisurely afternoon with guests when you prepare this updated classic ahead of time.

Prep time: 35 minutes
Bake time: 1 hour
Stand time: 15 minutes

10 uncooked lasagna noodles

1 jar (16 ounces) white Alfredo pasta sauce

1/4 cup milk

1 1/2 teaspoons dried oregano leaves

3 cups coarsely chopped cooked chicken

1 can (14 ounces) artichoke hearts in water, drained and chopped

1/2 cup chopped red bell pepper

1/4 cup finely chopped onion

1 garlic clove, pressed

3 cups (12 ounces) shredded mozzarella cheese

1 package (4 ounces) crumbled feta cheese

2 cups packed fresh baby spinach leaves (about 4 ounces)

1. Preheat oven to 375°F. Cook noodles in **Professional (8-qt.) Stockpot** according to package directions, using shortest cook time; drain. In **Small Batter Bowl**, combine Alfredo sauce, milk and oregano. Whisk until blended using **Stainless Steel Whisk**; set aside.

2. Coarsely chop chicken with **Chef's Knife**. Using **Food Chopper**, chop artichokes, bell pepper and onion; place in large (4-qt.) **Colander Bowl**. Press garlic over bowl using **Garlic Press**. Add mozzarella and feta cheeses; mix well.

3. To assemble lasagna, spread 2/3 cup of the Alfredo sauce mixture over bottom of **Rectangular Baker**. Top with half of the noodles, overlapping to fit. Layer half of the spinach leaves over noodles; top with half of the chicken mixture. Repeat layers, starting with half of the remaining sauce. After layering, pour remaining sauce over top of lasagna.

4. Cover baker with aluminum foil. Bake 45 minutes. Carefully remove foil. Continue baking 10-15 minutes or until bubbly. Remove from oven; let stand 15 minutes for easier serving. Cut into squares; serve using **Large Serving Spatula.**

Yield: 12 servings

Nutrients per serving: Calories 320, Total Fat 16 g, Saturated Fat 9 g, Cholesterol 80 mg, Carbohydrate 21 g, Protein 24 g, Sodium 780 mg, Fiber 2 g
Diabetic exchanges per serving: 1 1/2 starch, 3 meat (1 1/2 carb)

Celebrate with Style

Celebrate the incomparable flavors in this colorful lasagna with a crisp green salad tossed with pink grapefruit and orange segments, red onion slices and a honey-lime vinaigrette. For dessert, nothing compares to *Creamy Lemon Supreme* (p. 109).

Cook's Tips

For added convenience, use a rotisserie-cooked chicken, available at most large supermarkets, for this recipe. One cooked chicken weighs about 2 pounds and will yield approximately 3 cups of chopped meat.

Prepare lasagna as recipe directs up to 1 day in advance. Cover with aluminum foil and refrigerate. When ready to bake, remove from refrigerator while preheating oven. Increase covered baking time to 55 minutes. Continue as recipe directs.

Sunrise Oven Omelet

The kids will have a chance to make Mom's day special when they treat her to this easy and tasty hot-from-the-oven omelet.

Prep time: 20 minutes
Bake time: 45-50 minutes
Stand time: 5 minutes

16 round miniature frozen homestyle waffles, thawed
³/₄ cup frozen chopped broccoli, thawed
¹/₂ cup chopped red bell pepper
¹/₄ cup green onions with tops, chopped
 1 cup (4 ounces) shredded cheddar cheese, divided
 1 cup (4%) small curd cottage cheese
¹/₄ cup all-purpose flour
 6 eggs, divided
¹/₃ cup milk
¹/₂ teaspoon salt
¹/₈ teaspoon ground black pepper

1. Thaw waffles at room temperature 10 minutes. Preheat oven to 375°F. Spray **Deep Dish Pie Plate** with nonstick cooking spray. Drain broccoli on paper towel. Chop bell pepper and green onions with **Food Chopper**. Combine broccoli, bell pepper, green onions and ³/₄ cup of the cheddar cheese in **Small Batter Bowl**; mix gently.

2. Sprinkle vegetable mixture evenly over bottom of pie plate. Arrange waffles, slightly overlapping, around edge of pie plate; press lightly into vegetable mixture.

3. In **Classic Batter Bowl**, vigorously whisk cottage cheese, flour and 1 egg using **Stainless Steel Whisk** until well blended. Whisk in remaining eggs, milk, salt and black pepper; pour over vegetable mixture.

4. Cover edge of waffles with 2- to 3-inch-wide strips of aluminum foil. Bake 45-50 minutes or until egg mixture is set. (A knife inserted near center will come out clean.) Remove from oven; sprinkle with remaining ¹/₄ cup cheddar cheese. Let stand 5 minutes. Cut into wedges and serve using **Slice 'N Serve®**.

Yield: 8 servings

Nutrients per serving: Calories 210, Total Fat 11 g, Saturated Fat 5 g, Cholesterol 185 mg, Carbohydrate 13 g, Protein 14 g, Sodium 520 mg, Fiber 1 g
Diabetic exchanges per serving: 1 starch, 1¹/₂ meat, ¹/₂ fat (1 carb)

Cook's Tips

*To thaw waffles, remove from freezer 10 minutes before using. If necessary, cut waffles apart using the **Serrated Bread Knife**.*

Substitute 4 round frozen homestyle waffles, thawed and cut into quarters, for the miniature waffles, if desired. Prepare as recipe directs.

Celebrate with Style

Kids love to help in the kitchen, especially when it involves an element of surprise. With a little help from an adult, they'll be able to put a simple menu together in no time. Include chilled orange juice, fresh berries or cut-up fruit, and warm muffins or bagels for a memorable Mother's Day treat.

Lemon-Dill Grilled Salmon & Asparagus

Sometimes the most elegant main dishes are the easiest to make. You'll find this to be the case when preparing simple grilled salmon steaks and fresh asparagus.

Prep time: 15 minutes
Marinating time:
  30-60 minutes
Grill time: 10-13 minutes

1   large lemon
1/2 cup olive oil
1/4 cup Dijon mustard
1   tablespoon Pantry All-Purpose
    Dill Mix
1/4 teaspoon salt
1   pound asparagus spears, trimmed
4   salmon steaks, cut 1 inch thick
    (about 6-8 ounces each)
    Lemon wedges and fresh dill weed
    (optional)

1. Zest lemon with **Lemon Zester/Scorer** to measure 1 teaspoon zest. Juice lemon using **Juicer** to measure 1/4 cup juice. In **Small Batter Bowl**, whisk together oil, mustard, juice, zest, dill mix and salt using **Stainless Steel Whisk**. Brush asparagus spears with 2 tablespoons of the marinade; set aside.

2. Reserve 1/4 cup of the marinade to brush over salmon while grilling. Place salmon steaks and remaining 3/4 cup marinade in resealable plastic food storage bag; turn to coat. Marinate in refrigerator 30-60 minutes, turning occasionally.

3. Prepare grill for direct cooking over medium coals. Place asparagus spears crosswise on grid of grill. Grill 9-10 minutes or until crisp-tender, turning frequently with **Barbecue Tongs**. Remove asparagus to serving platter; cover to keep warm.

4. Lightly grease grid of grill. Drain salmon; discard marinade. Place salmon on grid. Brush with half of the reserved marinade using **Barbecue Basting Brush**. Cover; grill 5 minutes. Turn using **Barbecue Turner**; brush with remaining marinade. Continue grilling, covered, 5-7 minutes or until salmon flakes easily with fork. Serve with asparagus. Garnish with lemon wedges and fresh dill weed, if desired.

Yield: 4 servings

Nutrients per serving: Calories 500, Total Fat 34 g, Saturated Fat 6 g, Cholesterol 85 mg, Carbohydrate 7 g, Protein 39 g, Sodium 470 mg, Fiber 3 g
Diabetic exchanges per serving: 1/2 starch, 5 meat, 2 fat (1/2 carb)

Cook's Tips

To trim asparagus, snap off and discard tough stem ends.

Dried dill weed can be substituted for the All-Purpose Dill Mix, if desired.

Don't marinate the salmon any longer than 60 minutes. If left in the marinade longer, the lemon juice will cause the fish to turn firm and opaque. And, of course, always marinate fish in the refrigerator.

Other medium-textured fish such as mahi-mahi, grouper, halibut or cod are well suited for this recipe. If using fillets, leave the skin on. To prevent the fish from sticking, start with a clean grill grid. Heat the grid 2-3 minutes over hot coals, then brush lightly with oil.

*For a pretty citrus garnish, use the **Lemon Zester/ Scorer** to score around a lemon before cutting it into wedges. The long strips of zest can be used as a garnish, too.*

Celebrate with Style

Have an intimate group on the patio to quietly celebrate a birthday or job promotion with style. For appetizers, prepare the olive mixture for *Warm Olive Bruschetta* (p. 16), but plan to serve this appetizer cold. (Guests can even assemble their own as you fire up the grill.) Cook a simple packaged couscous or rice mix, slice garden-fresh tomatoes and serve the guest of honor's favorite dessert.

Grilled Asian Pork Tenderloin Salad

Dazzle guests with this refreshing main dish salad that plays on the complex flavor of our Asian Seasoning Mix. Slice the pork tenderloins into medallions for an attractive presentation.

Prep time: 30 minutes
Grill time: 25-35 minutes

Cook's Tips

Most of the ingredients for this salad can be prepared 1 day ahead. Prepare dressing, cover and refrigerate. Wash salad greens, wrap in damp paper towels, place in resealable plastic food storage bags and refrigerate. Prepare vegetables, place in separate containers and refrigerate. Even the pork tenderloin can be grilled the day before. After grilling, cool whole tenderloin 30 minutes before wrapping and placing in the refrigerator. Cut into slices when you're ready to assemble the salad.

Pork tenderloins are commonly found packaged in vacuum packs. Most often, 2 pork tenderloins, weighing 12-16 ounces each, come in each vacuum pack for a combined weight of approximately 2 pounds.

*To toast almonds, place in **Small (8-in.) Sauté Pan** and heat over medium-high heat until light golden brown, stirring constantly. Remove nuts from pan and cool completely.*

Dressing

- 1/3 **cup rice vinegar**
- 3 **tablespoons soy sauce**
- 4 **teaspoons Pantry Asian Seasoning Mix**
- 2 **teaspoons sugar**
- 3/4 **cup vegetable oil**

Salad

- 3 **tablespoons Pantry Asian Seasoning Mix**
- 1 **tablespoon vegetable oil**
- 2 **pork tenderloins (about 1 pound each)**
- 10 **cups mixed salad greens (about 1 1/4 pounds)**
- 1 1/2 **cups sugar snap peas, cut in half diagonally**
- 1 **medium red bell pepper, cut into 2-inch strips**
- 1/2 **red onion, sliced into thin wedges**
- 1/3 **cup shredded carrot**
- 1/4 **cup slivered almonds, toasted**

1. For dressing, combine rice vinegar, soy sauce, seasoning mix, sugar and vegetable oil in **Small Batter Bowl**. Mix well using **Stainless Steel Whisk**. Cover; refrigerate until ready to use.

2. For salad, prepare grill for indirect cooking over medium coals. Combine seasoning mix and vegetable oil; rub over surface of pork. Grill pork, covered 25-35 minutes, turning every 10 minute using **Barbecue Tongs** until **Pocket Thermometer** registers 155°F for medium doneness; 165°F for well done. Remove pork from grill; let stand 5 minutes. (Temperature will rise approximately 5°F during standing to reach the desired temperatures of 160°F for medium doneness and 170°F for well done.) Carve into thin slices using **Carving Set**.

3. Arrange salad greens on large serving platter; top with sugar snap peas, red bell pepper, red onion and carrot. Sprinkle with toasted almonds. Arrange tenderloin slices around edge of platter. Serve salad using **3-Way Tongs**. Drizzle with 1 cup dressing; refrigerate remaining dressing.

Yield: 8 servings

Nutrients per serving (1 1/2 cups salad, 3 ounces pork, 2 tablespoons dressing): Calories 390, Total Fat 24 g, Saturated Fat 2.5 g, Cholesterol 65 mg, Carbohydrate 14 g, Protein 27 g, Sodium 310 mg, Fiber 3 g

Diabetic exchanges per serving (1 1/2 cups salad, 3 ounces pork, 2 tablespoons dressing): 1 starch, 3 meat, 2 fat (1 carb)

Grilled Italian Sausages with Confetti Vegetable Relish

Prep time: 30 minutes
Grill time: 4-6 minutes

Your 4th of July will sizzle with these tasty sausages topped with a zesty Italian-style relish. Bratwurst sausages work equally well in these hearty sandwiches.

2 bottles (12 ounces each) non-alcoholic beer
1 medium onion, cut into wedges
10-12 Italian sausages (about 3 pounds)
1 medium green bell pepper, cut into 4 wedges
1 medium red bell pepper, cut into 4 wedges
10-12 submarine or bratwurst rolls, split
1/2 cup mild giardiniera relish in vegetable oil
1/4 cup Dijon mustard

1. Prepare grill for cooking at medium temperature. Combine non-alcoholic beer and onion in **Family (12-in.) Skillet**. Prick sausages several times. Place sausages in beer; bring to a boil. Reduce heat; cover and simmer 10-15 minutes or until sausages are no longer pink. Remove sausages from beer. Strain onion using small **Colander**; discard beer. Reserve onion.

2. Place sausages and bell peppers on grid of grill. Grill, covered, 4-6 minutes or until sausages are evenly browned and bell peppers are tender, turning occasionally with **Barbecue Tongs**. Remove sausages and bell peppers from grill; keep sausages warm.

3. Place buns, cut side down, on grill. Grill 30-60 seconds or until lightly toasted; keep warm.

4. Chop reserved onion and bell peppers with **Food Chopper**. Combine onion, bell peppers and giardiniera relish in **Small Batter Bowl**; mix gently. Place sausages in buns. Top with vegetable relish and mustard.

Yield: 10-12 servings

Nutrients per serving (1 sandwich): Calories 440, Total Fat 22 g, Saturated Fat 9 g, Cholesterol 50 mg, Carbohydrate 38 g, Protein 21 g, Sodium 1130 mg, Fiber 3 g
Diabetic exchanges per serving: 2 1/2 starch, 2 meat, 2 fat (2 1/2 carb)

Celebrate with Style

Complete the menu for your backyard barbecue with *Southern-Style Salsa* (p. 35), *Picnic Potato Salad* (p. 80), grilled corn on the cob, ice-cold watermelon wedges and *All-American Celebration Cake* (p. 116). Wrap plastic eating utensils in red, white and blue paper napkins, tie with raffia and place in the **Tool Turn-About** for easy access. Decorate the center compartment with flags and miniature pom pons for a festive touch.

Cook's Tips

Giardiniera relish is a jarred condiment that has a mixture of finely chopped vegetables, Italian spices, vinegar and oil. It can be found in the Italian foods section or deli department of your supermarket.

Giardiniera, made with vegetables cut in large pieces, can also be used. Just finely chop the vegetables.

If using a product packed in water, drain and finely chop the vegetables. Add 1 tablespoon vegetable oil and mix gently. If using a product packed in oil, finely chop the vegetables. No additional oil is necessary.

To save time on the day of a picnic, cook the sausages as directed in Step 1 up to 2 days in advance. Cover and refrigerate sausages and onion. When ready to serve, continue from Step 2 as recipe directs except increase grilling time for sausages to 10-12 minutes.

Picnic Potato Salad

Potato salad gets a lift of flavor with ready-made onion dip. It's easy, delicious and so much better than the traditional deli version.

Prep time: 20 minutes
Cook time: 8-10 minutes
Chill time: 2 hours

3   **pounds small red potatoes, cut into 1-inch cubes**

2 1/2   **teaspoons salt, divided**

1   **cup sliced celery**

1/2   **cup chopped red onion**

4   **hard-cooked eggs**

1   **cup refrigerated French onion dip**

1   **tablespoon packed brown sugar**

1/4   **teaspoon coarsely ground black pepper**

  Celery leaves and red onion wedges (optional)

1. Place potatoes in **Professional (4-qt.) Casserole**. Cover potatoes with water; add 1 teaspoon of the salt. Cover; bring to a boil and cook 8-10 minutes or until tender. Drain using large **Colander**; cool completely.

2. Slice celery using **Chef's Knife**. Chop onion and 3 of the eggs using **Food Chopper**.

3. Combine onion dip, brown sugar, remaining 1 1/2 teaspoons salt and black pepper in large **Colander Bowl**. Add potatoes, celery, onion and chopped eggs; mix gently with **Mix 'N Scraper®**. Cover with lid; refrigerate at least 2 hours or overnight.

4. Transfer salad to chilled **Chillzanne® Bowl**. To serve, slice remaining egg with **Egg Slicer Plus®**; place on top of salad. Garnish with celery leaves and red onion wedges, if desired.

Yield: 12 servings

Nutrients per serving: Calories 160, Total Fat 4 g, Saturated Fat 2.5 g, Cholesterol 85 mg, Carbohydrate 24 g, Protein 5 g, Sodium 620 mg, Fiber 2 g
Diabetic exchanges per serving: 1 1/2 starch, 1 fat (1 1/2 carb)

Cook's Tips

Cool drained potatoes in colander quickly by placing under cold running water.

This potato salad can be prepared up to 1 day in advance.

To keep salads cold for picnics or potlucks, transfer salad that has been chilled overnight into a chilled Chillzanne® Bowl. The bowl contains a unique food-safe gel that keeps foods cold for hours. For best results, place the bowl in the freezer for at least 4 hours or overnight before using.

Chicken Pesto Sandwich Ring

Bistro-style ingredients and ring-shaped French bread make this sandwich ideal for an evening concert under the stars.

Prep time: 30 minutes
Bake time: 26-30 minutes
Grill time: 12-15 minutes

Cook's Tips

Spoonable salad dressing is a jarred dressing similar to mayonnaise. It is thick, creamy, but contains no egg yolks, and has a slightly sweeter taste.

The Chillzanne® Platter *is perfect for toting this sandwich to a picnic or patio party. Cut sandwich into wedges and use long party picks to secure before placing on chilled platter. Cover with dome lid and snap the handle over the lid and platter.*

Avoid last minute rushing with some easy make-ahead steps. A day before the picnic, bake bread, cool completely, wrap tightly and store at room temperature. Chicken and bell pepper slices can be cooked the day before, too. Store them covered in the refrigerator. On the day of the picnic, you can assemble the sandwich up to 6 hours in advance. Just refrigerate uncut and covered.

2 packages (11 ounces each) refrigerated French bread dough

2 tablespoons olive oil, divided

3 tablespoons grated fresh Parmesan cheese

1 pound boneless, skinless chicken breasts
  Salt and ground black pepper

2 medium red bell peppers

2/3 cup spoonable salad dressing (see Cook's Tips)

1/3 cup prepared basil pesto

1/4 teaspoon Pantry Lemon Pepper Seasoning Mix

2 cups fresh spinach leaves, washed and stemmed

1. Preheat oven to 350°F. Place dough, seam side down, on **Large Round Stone**. Join ends of dough together to form 1 large ring.

2. Using **Serrated Bread Knife**, make 8 diagonal cuts, 1/2-inch deep, on top of dough. Using **Pastry Brush**, lightly brush dough with 2 teaspoons of the olive oil. Sprinkle with cheese. Bake 26-30 minutes or until deep golden brown. Immediately remove bread to **Cooling Rack**; cool completely.

3. Prepare grill for cooking at medium temperature. Brush chicken with 1 teaspoon of the remaining olive oil; season lightly with salt and black pepper. Slice bell peppers into 1/2-inch-thick strips; toss with remaining 1 tablespoon olive oil in **Classic Batter Bowl**. Place chicken and bell peppers on grid of grill. Grill uncovered, 12-15 minutes or until chicken is no longer pink in the center and bell pepper strips are tender, turning occasionally using **Barbecue Tongs**; remove from grill; cool slightly.

4. Cut chicken into thin slices. Combine salad dressing, pesto and seasoning mix.

5. To assemble sandwich, cut bread in half horizontally with **Serrated Bread Knife**. Using **Small Spreader**, spread half of the pesto mixture over cut side of bread bottom; cover with spinach leaves. Arrange sliced chicken evenly over spinach; top with bell pepper strips. Spread remaining pesto mixture over cut side of bread top; place over bottom half. Cut into 8 wedges with serrated bread knife.

Yield: 8 servings

Nutrients per serving: Calories 430, Total Fat 21 g, Saturated Fat 5 g, Cholesterol 45 mg, Carbohydrate 37 g, Protein 22 g, Sodium 740 mg, Fiber 2 g
Diabetic exchanges per serving: 2 1/2 starch, 2 meat, 2 fat (2 1/2 carb)

Celebrate with Style

Add *Calypso Peach Salsa* (p. 34), tortilla chips and crinkle-cut melon slices to your picnic basket. Pack *Coconut Almond Brownie Squares* (p. 102) for a deliciously decadent dessert.

Sweet Endings

A dazzling display of delightful, delectable, dream-come-true desserts

All-Occasion Cookies (p. 86-89)

All-Occasion Cookies

*Create cookies for any occasion with one simple cookie dough and a host
of fabulous flavor variations and decorating ideas.*

1 **package (18.25 ounces) white cake mix**

2³/4 **cups all-purpose flour**

1 **pound (4 sticks) butter or margarine, divided
(do not use vegetable oil spread)**

Milk or beaten egg white (optional)

**Optional decorations: colored sugar crystals,
sprinkles, chopped nuts, *Decorator Icing*
(p. 88), *Melted Chocolate* (p. 88) or
powdered sugar**

1. Preheat oven to 350°F. In **Small Batter Bowl**,
microwave 2 sticks of the butter on HIGH 1 minute
or until melted. Slice remaining butter into ¹/2-inch
pieces; add to melted butter, tossing to coat. Allow
butter to stand 3-5 minutes or until softened.

2. Meanwhile, in large bowl, combine cake mix and
flour; blend well using **Stainless Steel Whisk**,
breaking up any large lumps. Whisk butter until
smooth and free of lumps. If necessary, microwave
butter an additional 10-20 seconds or until creamy
and pourable. *Do not melt completely.*

3. Pour butter all at once into dry ingredients, scraping
butter from batter bowl. Mix until dry ingredients are
incorporated and dough is smooth. (If dough is too
stiff to stir, knead by hand until smooth.)

4. Form cookies as desired (see p. 87). To decorate
cookies *before* baking, brush unbaked cookies lightly
with milk or egg white using **Pastry Brush** and
sprinkle with colored sugar crystals, sprinkles or finely
chopped nuts.

5. Bake cookies on flat **Baking Stone** 15-17 minutes or
until very light golden brown. Cool 3 minutes on
baking stone; remove to **Cooling Rack**. Cool
completely. To decorate cookies *after* baking, use
Decorator Icing or *Melted Chocolate*, or sprinkle with
powdered sugar using **Flour/Sugar Shaker.**

Nutrients per serving (2 undecorated cookies, 0.5 ounces each): Calories 130,
Total Fat 8 g, Saturated Fat 5 g, Cholesterol 20 mg, Carbohydrate 13 g, Protein 1 g,
Sodium 140 mg, Fiber less than 1 g
Diabetic exchanges per serving (1 cookie): 1 starch, 1¹/2 fat (1 carb)

Flavor Variations

Chocolate Cookies: Substitute one package (18.25
ounces) devil's food cake mix for the white cake mix.

Peanut Butter Cookies: Substitute one package
(18.25 ounces) yellow cake mix for the white cake
mix. Add ²/3 cup peanut butter to softened butter in
Step 2; whisk until smooth. Add to dry ingredients as
directed is Step 3.

Spice Cookies: Substitute one package (18.25 ounces)
yellow cake mix for the white cake mix and add 1
tablespoon **Pantry Cinnamon Plus™ Spice Blend.**

Forming Cookies

Pressed cookies: Fill **Cookie Press**, fitted with disk of your choice, with dough. Press dough onto flat Baking Stone, 1 inch apart. Yield: about 8 dozen cookies.

Cutout cookies: Turn dough out onto well-floured **Cutting Board**. With floured hands, gently knead dough, adding up to ½ cup additional flour as needed to form a firm dough. Divide dough into 3 equal portions. Shape each portion of dough into an 8-inch disk. Generously flour surface of cutting board or counter top. Roll one disk of dough out evenly to ⅛-inch thickness using **Baker's Roller™**. Cut cookie shapes using **Bread Tubes**; transfer to flat Baking Stone, 1 inch apart. Yield: about 2½ dozen cookies.

Drop cookies: If desired, stir ½ to 1 cup (any combination) of the following ingredients into the dough: chocolate morsels or or miniature candy-coated chocolate pieces; toffee bits; chopped nuts or candies; or dried fruit. Using **Small Scoop**, drop level scoops of cookie dough onto flat Baking Stone, 2 inches apart. Yield: about 7 dozen cookies.

Color Variations

Tinted cookies: Add food color, one drop at a time, to mixed dough in Step 3. Knead into dough until desired color is achieved.

Marbled cookies: Add food color, one drop at a time, to mixed dough in Step 3. Knead just until color streaks throughout the dough.

Multi-colored pressed cookies: Divide dough into 2 or 3 portions. Tint dough as directed for tinted cookies to make 2 or 3 contrasting colors of dough. Roll each color into a 1-inch thick log; place side by side and form into one large log. Place log into barrel of **Cookie Press**. Form and bake as directed for pressed cookies.

Decorating Techniques with Icing and Chocolate

Prepare Decorator Icing *or* Melted Chocolate *(see below)*. Frost cookies with icing using **Small Spatula**, *if desired*. Make piping bag *(see below)* and drizzle or pipe icing or melted chocolate in decorative designs over baked cookies.

Decorator Icing

3 cups powdered sugar

1 tablespoon meringue powder (see Cook's Tips)

5-6 tablespoons warm water

Food coloring (optional)

1. Combine powdered sugar and meringue powder in Classic Batter Bowl. Add 5 tablespoons water; mix well. Add water, 1 teaspoon at a time, mixing well after each addition until of desired consistency.

2. Add food coloring, one drop at a time, until desired color is reached.

3. Decorate cookies as desired. Icing will dry hard in 1-2 hours. Yield: $1^1/2$ cups

Melted Chocolate

2 squares (1 ounce each) semi-sweet chocolate for baking or $^1/2$ cup semi-sweet chocolate morsels

1. Place chocolate in **Small Micro-Cooker®**. Microwave, uncovered, on HIGH $1\text{-}1^1/2$ minutes, stirring after each 20-second interval or until melted and smooth. Do not overheat.

To make piping bag: Place a small, resealable plastic food storage bag inside **Measure-All® Cup**. Pour icing or melted chocolate into corner of bag. Twist top of bag; secure with **Twixit! Clip**. Cut a small tip off corner of bag to allow icing or chocolate to flow through.

Drizzling technique: Transfer cooled cookies onto **Cooling Rack**. Place cooling rack over a piece of **Parchment Paper** to catch drippings. Using piping bag, drizzle icing or melted chocolate over cookies; let stand until set.

Piping technique: Using piping bag, pipe icing or melted chocolate onto cooled cookies. Try following the pattern on pressed cookies or, create your own designs on cutout cookies. When using more than one color, make sure to allow the first color to set completely before using a second color or the colors will bleed.

Drag-through designs *(pictured on p. 89)*: Spread cooled cutout cookie with icing, forming a smooth surface. Immediately squeeze drops of contrasting colored icing from piping bag onto surface of wet icing. Drag **Cake Tester** through the drops of icing to form a heart shape.

Specialty Cookies

Chocolate Kiss Cookies: Top baked pressed or drop cookies, straight from the oven, with chocolate candy kisses.

Cutout Cookie Sandwiches: Cut flower shapes from dough using **Scalloped Bread Tube**. Cut out the center of half of the cookies using The **Corer™**. Bake as directed for cutout cookies. When cool, spread the back of one of the solid cookies with 1 tablespoon jam or frosting. Make a sandwich using one of the cookies with the hole in the center, allowing the filling to show through. Lightly dust cookies with powdered sugar.

Thumbprint Cookies: Roll 1-inch balls of cookie dough between palms of hands until smooth. Place on **Parchment Paper**. Make a deep indentation in center. Bake as directed. Pipe prepared frostings, peanut butter or jam into cooled cookies using **Easy Accent® Decorator**. Decorate with sliced almonds or chopped nuts.

Cook's Tips

- *Make sure to preheat the oven 10-15 minutes before baking.*

- *When making these cookies, do not substitute vegetable oil spreads for the butter or margarine. The added water in these products can cause cookies to be flat and thin with a tough texture.*

- *The first batch of cookies baked on a baking stone may require a slightly longer bake time. After the first batch, the time range indicated in the recipe should yield good results.*

- *If you have only one baking stone, portion the cookie dough onto* **Parchment Paper**, *cut to the size of the baking stone. As you remove one batch of cookies from the oven, the unbaked cookies on parchment can be quickly placed onto the baking stone and into the oven. This will save preparation time and make cleanup easier, too.*

- *For best results, let cookies remain on baking stone 2-3 minutes before transferring to* **Cooling Rack** *using* **Mini-Serving Spatula** *or* **Large Spatula**. *This standing time allows the sugars to become firm and prevents cookies from breaking or wrinkling.*

- *More than one batch of cookies can be baked at the same time. For best results, position the baking stones on separate oven racks but not directly above one another. Rotate the baking stones halfway through the baking time to ensure evenly baked cookies.*

- *Meringue powder (which contains pasteurized egg whites) is packaged in cans and can be found in stores that carry cake decorating supplies. Icing that has meringue powder in it will become smooth and hard once it has dried.*

- *To make cutout cookies into hanging ornaments, or to use as gift tags, poke a hole near the top of cookies with a small drinking straw before baking. Repeat immediately after baking if the hole closes. Insert a narrow ribbon through the hole and tie the ends in a knot.*

- *To store cookies, cool completely, then place cookies in a tightly covered container. For longer storage, freeze up to 1 month. To thaw, let the cookies stand at room temperature for 15 minutes.*

- *Separate frosted or decorated cookies between layers of Parchment Paper or waxed paper.*

- *To package cookies for gift-giving, line a cardboard gift box or decorative tin with tissue paper or plastic wrap. Carefully arrange cookies in the box, placing heavier cookies on the bottom. Place a sheet of parchment paper or tissue between layers of decorated cookies to keep them from sticking to each other. Decorate the package with festive ribbon and attach a gift tag.*

Harvest Honey Cake

*Honey cake, a traditional East European dessert, is eaten at joyful celebrations,
especially Rosh Hashanah to ensure a sweet new year.*

Cake

- 3 cups all-purpose flour
- 2 teaspoons Pantry Cinnamon Plus™ Spice Blend
- 1 teaspoon baking powder
- 1 teaspoon baking soda
- 3/4 teaspoon salt
- 2 cups chopped peeled Granny Smith apples (about 2 medium)
- 1 orange
- 3 eggs
- 1 cup granulated sugar
- 3/4 cup honey
- 3/4 cup vegetable oil
- 1/2 cup brewed coffee, cooled

Candied Orange Strips & Glaze

- 1 orange
- 1/2 cup plus 2 tablespoons granulated sugar
- 1/2 cup water

Frosting (see Cook's Tips)

1. Preheat oven to 325°F. Spray **Stoneware Fluted Pan** with nonstick cooking spray. For cake, combine flour, spice blend, baking powder, baking soda and salt in **Small Batter Bowl**; set aside.

2. Peel, core and slice apples with **Apple Peeler/Corer/Slicer**. Chop apples. Zest orange using **Lemon Zester/Scorer** to measure 2 teaspoons zest.

3. In **Classic Batter Bowl**, beat eggs on medium speed of electric mixer to blend. Add sugar, honey, oil and coffee; beat until smooth. Add flour mixture; beat just until combined. Fold in apples and zest using **Mix 'N Scraper®**. Pour into pan.

4. Bake 1 hour, 10 minutes to 1 hour, 15 minutes or until **Cake Tester** inserted near center comes out clean.

5. Meanwhile, for candied orange strips and glaze, remove zest from orange in long strips with scoring side of Lemon Zester/Scorer. Bring 1/2 cup sugar and water to boil in **Small (2-qt.) Saucepan** over medium-high heat, stirring occasionally. Add zest; reduce heat and simmer 9-10 minutes or until zest is translucent. Remove zest with fork to **Cooling Rack**; reserve syrup. Roll zest in remaining sugar; let dry.

6. Cool cake in pan 10 minutes. Loosen from sides and center tube. Invert onto cooling rack placed on wax paper. Glaze cake while hot by brushing with reserved syrup. Cool completely. To frost cake, see Cook's Tips.

Yield: 16 servings

Nutrients per serving: Calories 340, Total Fat 11 g,
Saturated Fat 1 g, Cholesterol 40 mg, Carbohydrate 60 g,
Protein 4 g, Sodium 230 mg, Fiber 1 g
Diabetic exchanges per serving: 1 starch, 3 fruit, 2 fat (4 carb)

Prep time: 50 minutes
Bake time: 1 hour,
   10 minutes to 1 hour,
   15 minutes
Cool time: 1 hour,
   10 minutes

Cook's Tips

Pumpkin pie spice can be substituted for Cinnamon Plus™ Spice Blend.

*When measuring flour, lightly stir the flour before filling the **Adjustable Measuring Scoop**, then level with the flat edge of a knife. Because flour has a tendency to settle and compact during storage, you'll end up with excess flour and tough, dry baked goods unless you stir it before measuring.*

*For frosting, combine 1 cup powdered sugar and enough orange juice (3-4 teaspoons) to make a thick frosting. Spread over top of cake using **Small Spreader**; top with candied orange strips. Cut cake into slices using **Slice 'N Serve®**.*

This cake can be made 1 day before the special celebration. Store tightly covered at room temperature.

French Apple Pastry

Baked on the Large Round Stone, this classic apple tart will impress the most discriminating guests – and it's easier than apple pie!

Prep time: 30 minutes
Bake time: 30-35 minutes
Cool time: 10 minutes

1 **package (15 ounces) refrigerated pie crusts (2 crusts)**

1 **cup toasted walnuts, finely grated**

5 **tablespoons sugar, divided**

2 **tablespoons all-purpose flour**

3 **medium red baking apples (about 1¼ pounds)**

1 **teaspoon Pantry Cinnamon Plus™ Spice Blend**

½ **cup apricot preserves**
  Vanilla ice cream (optional)

1. Preheat oven to 400°F. Let pie crusts stand at room temperature 15 minutes. Grate walnuts into **Small Batter Bowl** using **Deluxe Cheese Grater**. Add 3 tablespoons of the sugar and flour; mix thoroughly and set aside.

2. Lightly dust **Large Round Stone** with small amount of additional flour. Unfold one pie crust and place in center of baking stone. Using **Kitchen Spritzer**, spray lightly with water. Unfold second pie crust and place over crust on baking stone, matching edges and pressing down to seal. Using **Baker's Roller™**, roll both crusts out together to edge of baking stone. Fold ½ inch of edge of crust under forming an even border. Using smooth end of pastry tool, form a decorative edge. Spray lightly with water.

3. Spread walnut mixture evenly over prepared crust. Using **Apple Peeler/Corer/Slicer**, core and slice apples, leaving peels on. Cut slices in half. Starting at outside edge of crust, arrange apple slices, slightly overlapping over nut mixture in a circular pattern. Fill center with slices to form a blossom shape.

4. Combine spice blend and remaining 2 tablespoons sugar in **Flour/Sugar Shaker**; sprinkle over apples. Bake 30-35 minutes or until apples are tender and crust is golden brown. Remove to **Cooling Rack**.

5. Microwave preserves in **Small Micro-Cooker®** on HIGH 30 seconds or until melted. Brush over apples and crust edge with **Pastry Brush**. Cool at least 10 minutes. Cut into wedges using **Chef's Knife**. Serve warm or at room temperature with ice cream, if desired.

Yield: 12 servings

Nutrients per serving: Calories 300, Total Fat 16 g, Saturated Fat 5 g, Cholesterol 7 mg, Carbohydrate 39 g, Protein 3 g, Sodium 140 mg, Fiber 2 g
Diabetic exchanges per serving: 1 starch, 1½ fruit, 3 fat (3 carb)

Cook's Tips

Ground cinnamon can be substituted for the Cinnamon Plus™ Spice Blend, if desired.

*To toast walnuts, preheat oven to 350°F. Place nuts on **Small Bar Pan**; bake 10-12 minutes or until nuts begin to brown.*

Frosty Pumpkin Dessert

The flavors of this frozen dessert may remind you of autumn, but after one taste, you'll want to serve it all year long.

Prep time: 30 minutes
Freeze time: 8 hours

32 gingersnap cookies, finely chopped (1 1/3 cups crumbs)

1/4 cup butter or margarine, melted

1 container (1/2 gallon) vanilla ice cream, divided

2 1/2 cups thawed, frozen whipped topping, divided

2/3 cup toffee bits

1 cup solid pack pumpkin

1/3 cup packed brown sugar

1 1/2 teaspoons Pantry Cinnamon Plus™ Spice Blend

1. Chop cookies with **Food Chopper**. Place butter in **Small Micro-Cooker®**; microwave on HIGH 30-40 seconds or until melted. Stir in crumbs. Firmly press crumb mixture onto bottom of **Springform Pan**. Place in freezer.

2. Scoop half of the ice cream into **Classic Batter Bowl** using **Ice Cream Dipper**. Place in refrigerator 10 minutes to soften.

3. Fold 1 cup of the whipped topping and toffee bits into softened ice cream just until blended. Spread evenly over crust using **All-Purpose Spreader**. Freeze until firm, about 1 hour.

4. Place remaining ice cream in refrigerator 10 minutes to soften. Meanwhile, mix pumpkin, brown sugar and spice blend in batter bowl. Scoop softened ice cream into pumpkin mixture. Mix just until blended. Spread evenly over ice cream layer. Freeze until firm, about 8 hours or overnight.

5. When ready to serve, place dessert in refrigerator 20 minutes for easier slicing. Fill **Easy Accent® Decorator** with remaining whipped topping. Run **Utility Knife** around outside of dessert; remove collar from springform pan. Smooth sides with spreader. Cut dessert into wedges. Garnish each serving with whipped topping and sprinkle with additional spice blend, if desired.

Yield: 16 servings

Nutrients per serving: Calories 320, Total Fat 17 g, Saturated Fat 10 g, Cholesterol 40 mg, Carbohydrate 39 g, Protein 4 g, Sodium 180 mg, Fiber less than 1 g
Diabetic exchanges per serving: 1 starch, 1 1/2 fruit, 3 fat (2 1/2 carb)

Cook's Tips

Toffee bits can be found in the baking aisle of most supermarkets.

Pumpkin pie spice can be substituted for the Cinnamon Plus™ Spice Blend, if desired.

This dessert can be made days in advance and frozen.

To make cutting this frozen dessert easier, dip the utility knife into warm water and wipe it dry after cutting each wedge.

Celebrate with Style

This delightful dessert fits any season but is especially well suited for a Thanksgiving feast. Serve with orange spiced tea or freshly brewed coffee.

Cherry Eggnog Tea Bread

This festive, cherry-studded quick bread is the ultimate treat whether served for a brunch, an afternoon tea or a simple dessert.

Prep time: 25 minutes
Bake time: 1 hour,
    15 minutes to 1 hour,
    20 minutes

Bread

3/4 cup maraschino cherries, chopped and well drained

2 1/4 cups all-purpose flour

1 1/2 teaspoons baking powder

3/4 teaspoon ground nutmeg

3/4 teaspoon salt

1 cup granulated sugar

3/4 cup butter or margarine, softened

3 eggs

1 cup eggnog

Glaze

1/2 cup powdered sugar

3-4 teaspoons eggnog

1/4 cup toasted sliced natural almonds

1. Preheat oven to 325°F. Spray bottom only of **Stoneware Loaf Pan** with nonstick cooking spray. Chop maraschino cherries using **Food Chopper**. Place cherries on paper towels; pat dry.

2. In **Small Batter Bowl**, combine flour, baking powder, nutmeg and salt; set aside. In **Classic Batter Bowl**, beat granulated sugar and butter on high speed of electric mixer until mixture is light and fluffy.

3. On medium speed, add eggs, one at a time, beating until blended. Add one third of the flour mixture, beating on low speed just until combined. Beat in half of the eggnog. Add another one third of the flour mixture, the remaining eggnog, and then the remaining flour mixture, beating after each addition just until combined. Gently stir cherries into batter; pour batter into pan.

4. Bake 1 hour, 15 minutes to 1 hour, 20 minutes or until **Cake Tester** inserted in center comes out clean and top is golden brown. Cool in pan 5 minutes. Loosen sides of loaf; remove from pan to **Cooling Rack**. Cool completely.

5. For glaze, mix powdered sugar and eggnog until smooth; drizzle half of mixture over cooled loaf. Sprinkle evenly with almonds. Drizzle remaining glaze over almonds. Cut into slices using **Serrated Bread Knife**.

Yield: 12 servings

Nutrients per serving: Calories 340, Total Fat 15 g, Saturated Fat 9 g, Cholesterol 95 mg, Carbohydrate 47 g, Protein 5 g, Sodium 350 mg, Fiber less than 1 g
Diabetic exchanges per serving: 2 starch, 1 fruit, 3 fat (3 carb)

Cook's Tips

To make well in advance, prepare tea bread as directed in Steps 1-4. Wrap securely; freeze up to 1 month. When ready to serve, thaw bread at room temperature; unwrap. Prepare glaze and drizzle over bread as recipe directs.

To toast almonds, place in **Small (8-in.) Sauté Pan** *and heat over medium heat until light golden brown, stirring constantly. Remove nuts from pan and cool completely.*

Celebrate the gift of friendship by giving a special homemade treat from your kitchen. Wrap the finished loaf in colorful cellophane and tie with a festive ribbon.

Candy Cane Coffee Cake

*Nothing will brighten your holiday gatherings more than
this warm, fruit-filled brunch bread.*

Prep time: 1 hour
Bake time: 20-23 minutes
Cool time: 15 minutes

Cook's Tips

*One 16-ounce package
of hot roll mix can be
substituted for the Pizza
Crust & Roll Mix,
if desired.*

*Dried fruit morsel blends
are found near the raisins
in most supermarkets.*

*It's important to use the
right temperature of liquids
when working with yeast.
If the milk is too cool, it
will not activate the yeast
but if it is too hot, it may
kill the yeast. By using the*
Pocket *or* **Digital
Thermometer** *to measure
the temperature of the
liquid, you can help ensure
recipe success.*

The **V-Shaped Cutter** *is
great for drizzling the glaze
over this coffee cake.*

Coffee Cake

- 1 **pouch (16 ounces) Pantry Pizza Crust & Roll Mix (including yeast packet)**
- 1/4 **cup granulated sugar**
- 2 **eggs**
- 3/4 **cup very warm milk (120°F-130°F)**
- 1/4 **cup butter or margarine, softened**
- 1/2 **cup pecans, chopped**
- 3/4 **cup dried fruit morsel blend (such as dried cranberries, apples and cherries)**
- 1/2 **cup cherry preserves**
- 1 **tablespoon water**

Glaze

- 3/4 **cup powdered sugar**
- 2-3 **teaspoons milk**

1. Preheat oven to 375°F. For coffee cake, combine pizza crust & roll mix, yeast packet and granulated sugar in **Classic Batter Bowl**. Using **Egg Separator**, separate 1 egg white from yolk; reserve white. Add milk, butter, whole egg and egg yolk to batter bowl. Stir until mixture forms a ball.

2. Turn dough out onto well-floured surface. With floured hands, knead dough 5 minutes. Sprinkle additional flour over surface as needed to reduce stickiness. Cover; let dough rest 5 minutes.

3. Chop pecans with **Food Chopper**; combine with fruit morsels in **Small Batter Bowl**. Place dough in center of lightly floured **Rectangle Stone**; roll into 12 x 15-inch rectangle with lightly floured **Baker's Roller™**. Using **Skinny Scraper**, spread preserves in 6-inch strip lengthwise down center of dough to within 1/4 inch of each end; sprinkle fruit mixture evenly over preserves.

4. Cut 1-inch-wide strips on each side of fruit filling to within 1/2 inch of filling. Lift strips of dough across filling to meet in center, twisting each strip one turn; pinch together in center to seal. Tuck ends up to seal. Lift and stretch one end of shaped dough using lightly floured **Large Serving Spatula**; curve to form cane. Cover; let rise in warm place 30 minutes.

5. Lightly beat reserved egg white with 1 tablespoon water; brush over dough using **Pastry Brush**. Bake 20-23 minutes or until deep golden brown.

6. For glaze, mix powdered sugar and milk until smooth; drizzle over warm coffee cake. Cool 15 minutes. Cut into 1-inch slices using **Serrated Bread Knife**.

Yield: 15 servings

Nutrients per serving: Calories 250, Total Fat 8 g,
Saturated Fat 2.5 g, Cholesterol 40 mg, Carbohydrate 42 g,
Protein 5 g, Sodium 330 mg, Fiber less than 1 g
Diabetic exchanges per serving: 2 starch, 1 fruit, 1 fat (3 carb)

Tuxedo Brownie Cups

Dressed-up and irresistible, these filled brownie cups just might become the life of the party.

Prep time: 35 minutes
Bake time: 14 minutes
  per batch
Cool time: 20 minutes
  per batch

Cook's Tips

It's best to use a nonstick cooking spray containing flour when baking these brownie cups. In a pinch, use a paper towel to grease muffin cups with shortening then sprinkle with all-purpose flour using the **Flour/Sugar Shaker**. *Tap off excess flour. Do not bake brownies in paper or foil muffin cup liners as they will stick to the liners.*

Brownie cups can be baked, cooled and stored in an airtight container at room temperature up to 1 day before filling. Don't make the white chocolate filling ahead of time. It becomes too firm when refrigerated and can't be piped with the decorator.

The **Medium Scoop** *is a handy tool for scooping dessert fillings, frostings and whipped topping into the decorator.*

For tips on garnishing with melted chocolate, see Decorating Techniques (p. 88).

1   package (19-21 ounces) fudge brownie mix (plus ingredients to make cake-like brownies)
2   squares (1 ounce each) white chocolate for baking
2   tablespoons milk
1   package (8 ounces) cream cheese, softened
1/4 cup powdered sugar
1   cup thawed, frozen whipped topping
1   pint small strawberries, sliced
    Orange zest, mint leaves and melted semi-sweet chocolate for baking (optional)

1. Preheat oven to 325°F. Spray cups of **Deluxe Mini-Muffin Pan** with nonstick cooking spray for baking. (See Cook's Tips.) Prepare brownie mix according to package directions for cake-like brownies. Using **Small Scoop**, place 1 level scoop of batter in each cup, filling cups 2/3 full. Bake 14 minutes or until edges are set. Do not overbake.

2. Remove pan to **Cooling Rack**. Immediately press tops of brownies with **Mini-Tart Shaper** to make indentation. Cool in pan 15 minutes. Loosen edges and gently remove brownies from pan. Cool completely. Wash pan, spray with cooking spray and repeat baking with remaining batter.

3. Microwave white chocolate and milk in **Small Micro-Cooker**®, uncovered, on HIGH 1 minute; stir until smooth. Cool slightly. In **Classic Batter Bowl**, combine cream cheese and powdered sugar; mix well. Gradually stir in white chocolate mixture until smooth. Fold in whipped topping.

4. Fill **Easy Accent**® **Decorator** fitted with closed star tip with cream cheese mixture. Pipe cream cheese mixture into cooled brownie cups. Slice strawberries using **Egg Slicer Plus**®; arrange on tops of brownie cups. Garnish with orange zest and mint leaves or drizzle with melted semi-sweet chocolate, if desired. Place in airtight container and refrigerate 1-3 hours before serving.

Yield: 4 dozen

Nutrients per serving (1 brownie cup): Calories 110, Total Fat 6 g, Saturated Fat 2 g, Cholesterol 20 mg, Carbohydrate 11 g, Protein 1 g, Sodium 50 mg, Fiber 0 g
Diabetic exchanges per serving (1 brownie cup): 1 starch, 1 fat (1 carb)

Coconut Almond Brownie Squares

Who could believe such decadence could come from a 5-ingredient shopping list?
Bake these easy, candy-like bars and find out for yourself.

Prep time: 10 minutes
Bake time: 36-41 minutes
Cool time: 3 hours

1 **package (19-21 ounces) fudge brownie mix (plus ingredients to make cake-like brownies)**

1 **package (10 ounces) sweetened flaked coconut (3³/₄ cups)**

1 **package (11.5 ounces) semi-sweet chocolate chunks**

1 **can (14 ounces) sweetened condensed milk (not evaporated milk)**

1 **package (2.25 ounces) sliced natural almonds (²/₃ cup)**

1. Preheat oven to 350°F. Spray **Stoneware Bar Pan** with nonstick cooking spray. Prepare brownie mix according to package directions for cake-like brownies in **Classic Batter Bowl**. Spread evenly in pan. Bake 16-18 minutes or until brownie is set. Do not overbake.

2. Layer coconut and chocolate chunks over brownie base. Pour sweetened condensed milk evenly over coconut and chocolate chunks. Sprinkle with almonds.

3. Bake 20-23 minutes or until edges of coconut are deep golden brown and almonds are lightly toasted. Cool completely on **Cooling Rack**. Cut into bars.

Yield: 24 bars

Nutrients per serving (1 bar): Calories 370, Total Fat 19 g, Saturated Fat 6 g, Cholesterol 35 mg, Carbohydrate 45 g, Protein 6 g, Sodium 130 mg, Fiber 2 g
Diabetic exchanges per serving (1 bar): 2 starch, 1 fruit, 3¹/₂ fat (3 carb)

Cook's Tips

One package (12 ounces) semi-sweet chocolate morsels can be substituted for the chocolate chunks.

These bars taste even better the next day. To store leftover bars, place in airtight container at room temperature.

Celebrate with Style

Whether you're saying thank you, happy holidays or welcome to the neighborhood, these elegant brownies make a heartfelt gift.

Dazzle Berry Pie

Raspberries and chocolate are the heart's desire in this dazzling pie.

/2 package (15 ounces) refrigerated
    pie crusts (one crust)
1   cup boiling water
1   package (3 ounces) raspberry
    gelatin
/3 cup seedless raspberry jam
2   squares (1 ounce each) semi-sweet
    chocolate for baking
1   container (8 ounces) sour cream
1   container (8 ounces) frozen
    whipped topping, thawed, divided
1/2 pint fresh raspberries (about
    1 cup), divided
    Powdered sugar

1. Preheat oven to 425°F. Let pie crust
stand at room temperature 15 minutes.
Gently unfold onto lightly floured
surface. Roll to an 11 1/2-inch circle
using floured **Baker's Roller™**. Place
crust in **Deep Dish Pie Plate**, pressing
dough into bottom and up sides. Prick
bottom and sides using pastry tool. Bake
10-12 minutes or until golden brown.
Cool completely.

2. Stir boiling water into gelatin in **Small
Batter Bowl**; stir at least 2 minutes until
completely dissolved. Add jam; stir until
smooth. Cool until gelatin begins to
thicken.

3. Place chocolate in **Small Micro-
Cooker®**; microwave, uncovered, on
HIGH 1-1 1/2 minutes, stirring after each
20-second interval or until chocolate is
melted and smooth. Pour chocolate into
small resealable plastic food storage bag;
twist top of bag and secure. Cut a small
tip off corner of bag to allow chocolate
to flow through. Pipe chocolate around
top edge of pie crust. Using remaining
chocolate, pipe 8 heart-shaped
decorations onto **Parchment Paper**;
refrigerate 15 minutes or until set.

4. Combine sour cream and 2 cups of the
whipped topping in **Classic Batter
Bowl**. Add gelatin mixture; whisk until
smooth with **Stainless Steel Whisk**.
Reserve 1/3 cup raspberries; set aside.
Sprinkle remaining raspberries evenly
over bottom of pie crust; pour filling
over berries. Chill at least 3 hours or
until set.

5. Fill **Easy Accent® Decorator** with
remaining whipped topping. Pipe
8 rosettes evenly around edge of pie.
Arrange chocolate heart decorations
between rosettes. Place reserved berries
in center. Lightly sprinkle pie with
powdered sugar using **Flour/Sugar
Shaker**. Cut into wedges and serve
using **Slice 'N Serve®**.

Yield: 8 servings

Nutrients per serving: Calories 380, Total Fat 19 g,
Saturated Fat 13 g, Cholesterol 30 mg, Carbohydrate 45 g,
Protein 3 g, Sodium 140 mg, Fiber 2 g
Diabetic exchanges per serving: 1 starch, 2 fruit, 4 fat (3 carb)

Prep time: 30 minutes
Bake time: 10-12 minutes
Cool time: 30 minutes
Chill time: 3 hours

Cook's Tips

*When placing pie crust in
the pie plate, evenly ruffle
edge of crust for picture-
perfect results. To keep
crust from slipping down
sides of pie plate during
baking, firmly press edge of
pie crust to fluted edge of
pie plate in several places.*

*To cool the gelatin mixture
quickly, place in chilled
Chillzanne® Mini-Bowl
or set over bowl of ice. Stir
frequently until gelatin is
cooled and slightly
thickened.*

*Garnishing desserts with
chocolate decorations is
elegant yet easy. To make
pretty decorations in a jiffy,
pipe melted chocolate into
desired shapes onto a
parchment paper-lined
Chillzanne® Platter that
has been chilled. In about
5 minutes, the decorations
will be ready.*

Chocolate Caramel Oatmeal Chews

These mouth-watering bars are rich and chewy with caramel, chocolate and nuts.

2 cups quick or old-fashioned oats
1¾ cups all-purpose flour, divided
¾ cup packed brown sugar
1 teaspoon baking soda
1 cup butter or margarine, melted
1 cup butterscotch caramel
   ice cream topping
½ cup chopped pecans
1 package (6 ounces) semi-sweet
   chocolate morsels

1. Preheat oven to 350°F. Spray **Rectangular Baker** with nonstick cooking spray. Combine oats, 1½ cups of the flour, brown sugar and baking soda in **Classic Batter Bowl**. Add butter; mix until crumbly. Reserve 1 cup crumb mixture. Press remaining crumb mixture onto bottom of baker. Bake 15 minutes.

2. Combine ice cream topping and remaining ¼ cup flour in **Small Batter Bowl**; whisk until smooth using **Stainless Steel Whisk**. Drizzle over bottom crust; carefully spread to edges using **Large Spreader**.

3. Combine pecans and reserved crumb mixture in small bowl. Sprinkle crumb mixture and chocolate morsels evenly over caramel mixture. Bake 15-18 minutes or until golden brown and bubbly. Remove to **Cooling Rack**. Cool completely. Cut into bars.

Yield: 24 bars

Nutrients per serving (1 bar): Calories 240, Total Fat 17 g, Saturated Fat 6 g, Cholesterol 20 mg, Carbohydrate 32 g, Protein 3 g, Sodium 160 mg, Fiber 1 g
Diabetic exchanges per serving (1 bar): 1 starch, 1 fruit, 3 fat (2 carb)

Prep time: 15 minutes
Bake time: 30-33 minutes
Cool time: 2 hours

Cook's Tips

The **Measure All® Cup** is ideal for measuring sticky ingredients like ice cream topping, honey or molasses. Its unique design allows you to push ingredients from the cup with little cleanup.

To store leftover bars, place in tightly covered container at room temperature.

These bars can be prepared and frozen up to 1 month. Wrap securely. When ready to serve, thaw bars at room temperature; unwrap.

Celebrate with Style

For a no-fuss way to impress guests, serve this casual dessert while still slightly warm with a scoop of vanilla ice cream.

Creamy Lemon Supreme

Light, lemony and luscious, this elegant dessert will look spectacular on your party table.

Prep time: 45 minutes
Cook time: 10-12 minutes
Chill time: 6 hours

Crust

- 12 lemon creme-filled sandwich cookies, finely chopped (1 1/2 cups)
- 3 tablespoons butter or margarine, melted
- 1 lemon

Filling

- 2 lemons
- 1 package (2.9 ounces) lemon cook and serve pudding and pie filling (not instant)
- 1/2 cup sugar
- 2 cups water, divided
- 2 egg yolks
- 1 tablespoon butter or margarine
- 2 packages (8 ounces each) cream cheese, softened
- 1/2 cup powdered sugar
- 1 container (8 ounces) frozen whipped topping, thawed, divided

1. Lightly spray **Springform Pan** with nonstick cooking spray. For crust, finely chop cookies using **Food Chopper**. Combine cookie crumbs and melted butter in **Small Batter Bowl**. Press crumb mixture into bottom of pan. Cut 6 thin slices from lemon; cut each slice in half. Place lemon halves against inside collar of pan with cut side touching crust. Refrigerate while preparing filling.

2. For filling, zest lemons to measure 1 1/2 teaspoons zest using **Lemon Zester/Scorer**. Using **Juicer**, juice lemons to measure 1/4 cup juice. Combine pudding mix, sugar, 1/4 cup of the water and egg yolks in **Small (2-qt.) Saucepan**; stir until blended. Stir in remaining 1 3/4 cups water. Cook over medium heat, stirring constantly until mixture comes to a full boil; remove from heat. Set aside 1/2 cup of the pudding; cool slightly. Whisk butter and lemon juice into remaining pudding in saucepan; cool 15 minutes, stirring twice.

3. In **Classic Batter Bowl**, combine cream cheese and powdered sugar; mix well. Whisk in reserved 1/2 cup lemon pudding and 1 teaspoon lemon zest. Fold in 2 cups whipped topping; spread over crust.

4. Stir remaining lemon pudding mixture and spoon evenly over cream cheese filling using **Mix 'N Scraper®**, spreading gently. Refrigerate at least 6 hours.

5. Run **Quikut Paring Knife** around sides of dessert; release collar from pan. Garnish with remaining whipped topping and lemon zest. Cut into wedges.

Yield: 12 servings

Nutrients per serving: Calories 390, Total Fat 24 g, Saturated Fat 15 g, Cholesterol 85 mg, Carbohydrate 36 g, Protein 4 g, Sodium 250 mg, Fiber 0
Diabetic exchanges per serving: 1 starch, 1 1/2 fruit, 5 fat (2 1/2 carb)

Cook's Tips

To soften cream cheese, microwave on HIGH 30 seconds.

Vanilla creme-filled sandwich cookies can be substituted for the lemon creme-filled cookies, if desired.

You can use the **Easy Accent® Decorator** to pipe a decorative border of whipped topping around the edge of this dessert.

To make a double lemon twist garnish, score lemon and cut two thin slices. Make one cut into each slice, just to the center. Twist slices and place together for a double effect.

Teatime Tartlets

Create the perfect dessert trio with these tiny tartlets complete with three luscious filling variations. (See p. 112)

(See p. 112)

Prep time: 25 minutes
Bake time: 16-18
Cook time: 5 minutes
Chill time: 1 hour

Pastry Shells

- 1/2 package (15 ounces) refrigerated pie crust (1 crust)

Lemon Filling

- 1 lemon
- 1/3 cup sugar
- 1 1/2 tablespoons cornstarch
- 1/8 teaspoon salt
- 1/2 cup water
- 1 tablespoon butter or margarine
- 3-4 drops yellow food coloring (optional)

Garnish

- 1 cup thawed, frozen whipped topping
  Fresh blueberries, raspberries or sliced strawberries

1. For pastry shells, preheat oven to 400°F. Allow pie crust to stand at room temperature 15 minutes.

2. Roll crust into a 12-inch circle using lightly floured **Baker's Roller™**. Using **Scalloped Bread Tube**, cut out 12 pastry pieces; press one into each cup of **Stoneware Muffin Pan**. Prick bottom of pastry with pastry tool. Bake 16-18 minutes or until golden brown. Let stand 5 minutes. Remove pastry shells from muffin pan to **Cooling Rack**; cool.

3. For filling, zest lemon with **Lemon Zester/Scorer** using short strokes to measure 1 teaspoon zest; juice lemon with **Juicer** to measure 3 tablespoons juice.

4. Combine sugar, cornstarch and salt in **Petite (1 1/2-qt.) Saucepan**. Using **Nylon Spiral Whisk**, stir in water. Bring to a boil over medium-high heat. Reduce heat; cook and stir 2 minutes. Remove from heat; stir in butter, zest and food coloring, if desired. Gradually stir in lemon juice.

5. Using **Small Scoop**, fill each pastry shell with generous scoop of lemon filling; spread evenly, if necessary.

6. For garnish, attach open star tip to **Easy Accent® Decorator**; fill with whipped topping. Garnish pastry shells with whipped topping and fresh blueberries, raspberries or sliced strawberries.

Yield: 12 tartlets

Nutrients per serving (1 tartlet): Calories 130, Total Fat 7 g, Saturated Fat 4 g, Cholesterol 10 mg, Carbohydrate 16 g, Protein less than 1 g, Sodium 100 mg, Fiber 0 g
Diabetic exchanges per serving: 1 starch, 1 fat (1 carb)

Cook's Tips

When using the scalloped bread tube to cut the pastry, start on the outside edge of the crust. Cut 9 pastry pieces as close to each other and to the edge as possible; then cut 3 pastry pieces from the center. If necessary, roll crust out just enough to accommodate the 3 center pieces.

The pastry shells can be made up to 1 day in advance. Store the cooled baked shells in a resealable plastic food storage bag or airtight container at room temperature.

Filled tarts can be made and garnished up to 8 hours in advance. Store covered in the refrigerator.

The curved end of the **Citrus Peeler** *is handy for gently removing the baked pastry shells from the muffin pan.*

Teatime Tartlet Variations:

Cheesecake Tartlets: Prepare pastry shells as recipe directs. In **Small Batter Bowl**, combine 1/2 cup cream cheese spread and 1 tablespoon softened butter or margarine; blend well. Stir in 1 tablespoon powdered sugar and 1/4 teaspoon vanilla. Whisk in 1/2 cup thawed, frozen whipped topping until well blended. Fill pastry shells and garnish as recipe directs.

Chocolate Tartlets: Prepare pastry shells as recipe directs. Place 1 1/2 cups thawed, frozen whipped topping and 1/2 cup semi-sweet chocolate morsels in **Small Micro-Cooker®**. Microwave on HIGH 45 seconds; stir until blended and smooth. Fill pastry shells and garnish as recipe directs.

Prep time: 1 hour,
  30 minutes
Bake time: 1 hour,
  10 minutes to 1 hour,
  15 minutes
Cool time: 3 hours

Cook's Tip

Purchase a special doll pick (top half of a doll attached to a stick) at craft stores or stores that carry cake decorating supplies. To make cake using an 11-inch fashion doll, prepare cakes and frosting as recipe directs. Wrap top of doll with ribbon; wrap legs with plastic wrap. Cut cake for bottom of skirt as directed. Cut a 1 1/2-inch hole in center of each cake to accommodate doll's legs. Frost sides and top of first cake (bottom of skirt); top with second cake. Frost second cake. Insert doll and complete decorating as recipe directs.

Bride-to-Be Party Cake

Shower her with best wishes and this memorable, dream-come-true bridal cake.
(Pictured on p. 110)

Cake
  2 packages (18.25 ounces each) yellow cake mix (plus ingredients to make cake)

Frosting
  1 package (2 pounds) powdered sugar (about 7 cups), divided
  1 cup butter or margarine, softened
  1/2 cup vegetable shortening
  1 tablespoon clear vanilla extract
  6-7 tablespoons milk, divided
      Food coloring (optional)

Decorations
      Doll pick cake decoration, 7 inches (see Cook's Tips)
      Ribbon, lace, tulle, straight pins and craft flowers
      Small candies (optional)

1. For cake, preheat oven to 325°F. Grease and flour **Classic Batter Bowl**. Prepare 1 cake mix according to package directions. Pour into batter bowl. Bake 1 hour, 10 minutes to 1 hour, 15 minutes or until **Cake Tester** inserted in center comes out clean. Remove to **Cooling Rack**. Cool 15 minutes. Run **Large Spreader** around outside of cake and gently turn out onto cooling rack, large end down. Cool 3 hours. Repeat with remaining cake mix to make a second cake.

2. For frosting, combine half of the powdered sugar with butter, shortening, vanilla and 3 tablespoons of the milk in large bowl. Beat with electric mixer until smooth. Add remaining powdered sugar. Beat until light and fluffy, adding more milk, 1 tablespoon at a time, as needed for good spreading consistency. Tint some of the frosting with food coloring, if desired.

3. To assemble cake, using **Serrated Bread Knife**, trim off rounded bottoms of cakes to level. Slice off 2 inches from bottom (large end) of one cake and arrange on serving platter to serve as bottom of doll's skirt. (Wrap and freeze unused top portion of first cake for later use, or frost and serve with *Bride-to-Be Party Cake*, if more servings are needed.)

4. Frost sides and top of cake on platter using **Small Spreader**; top with second cake. Frost second cake. Wrap top of doll with ribbon or lace; secure in back with pins. Insert doll into cake. Fill **Easy Accent® Decorator** with frosting; decorate skirt as desired. Add small candies, if desired. Fashion veil with lace or tulle; attach to doll's head. Add flower bouquet. Refrigerate cake until ready to serve. To serve, remove doll and cut into slices with serrated bread knife.

Yield: 16 servings

Nutrients per serving: Calories 640, Total Fat 30 g, Saturated Fat 10 g, Cholesterol 85 mg, Carbohydrate 90 g, Protein 4 g, Sodium 420 mg, Fiber 0
Diabetic exchanges per serving: 1 starch, 5 fruit, 6 fat (6 carb)

Party Cake Variation:

Birthday Blastoff Cake: Prepare cakes and frosting as recipe directs. Tint approximately 1 1/2 cups of the frosting orange and 1/2 cup of the frosting blue. Slice off 2 inches from bottom (large end) of one cake and place on 14-inch round serving platter. (Reserve unused top for later use.) Frost bottom portion of cake with orange frosting using **Small Spreader**. Top with second cake; frost with white frosting. Using sharp scissors, cut flame shapes from fruit snack roll-ups and place on frosting. Attach 4 sugar cones to sides of cake. (Depending on shape of cone, it may be necessary to shave top edge of cone to fit snugly against cake, or simply push cone into cake.) Place space action figure on top of cake. Frost back of a 9-ounce clear plastic drinking glass. Place over toy figure. Frost sugar cone with white frosting; decorate with colored sprinkles. Attached to glass with frosting. Decorate cake with remaining frosting using **Easy Accent® Decorator** and small candies, as desired. Use red decorating gel to write birthday message, if desired.

Peanut Butter Rocky Road Dessert

Dad will never be as proud as when he's served this frozen treat topped with his favorite flavors – peanut butter and chocolate.

Prep time: 25 minutes
Bake time: 8 minutes
Cool time: 1 hour
Freeze time: 6 hours or
  overnight

5   peanut butter cup candies
    (0.6 ounces each), each cut
    into eighths
1 1/4   cups chocolate graham cracker
    crumbs (about eight
    5 x 2 1/4-inch crackers)
4   tablespoons butter or margarine,
    melted
2 1/2   cups cold milk
1   package (3.4 ounces)
    butterscotch instant pudding and
    pie filling
1   package (3.4 ounces) vanilla
    instant pudding and pie filling
1/4   cup peanut butter
1   container (8 ounces) frozen
    whipped topping, thawed
1/2   cup miniature marshmallows
1/4   cup peanuts
2   tablespoons chocolate-flavored
    syrup

1. Preheat oven to 350°F. Refrigerate peanut butter cup candies for easier cutting. Finely chop graham crackers using **Food Chopper**; place in **Small Batter Bowl**. Add butter; mix well. Press crumb mixture onto bottom of **Square Baker**. Bake 8 minutes. Cool completely.

2. Pour milk into **Classic Batter Bowl**. Add pudding mixes and peanut butter; whisk 2 minutes or until pudding begins to thicken using **Stainless Steel Whisk**. Fold in whipped topping. Spread evenly over crust.

3. Cut peanut butter cup candies into eighths using **Utility Knife**. Sprinkle candies, marshmallows and peanuts evenly over pudding mixture. Drizzle with chocolate syrup. Cover with aluminum foil; freeze 6 hours or overnight.

4. When ready to serve, let stand at room temperature 20 minutes. Cut dessert into squares using **Utility Knife** dipped in warm water.

Yield: 12 servings

Nutrients per serving: Calories 310, Total Fat 16 g,
Saturated Fat 8 g, Cholesterol 15 mg, Carbohydrate 38 g,
Protein 5 g, Sodium 380 mg, Fiber less than 1 g
Diabetic exchanges per serving: 2 starch, 1/2 fruit,
3 fat (2 1/2 carb)

Cook's Tips

When making crumb crusts for desserts, you'll find that the Food Chopper is a great tool for chopping graham crackers and cookies.

You can substitute 10 miniature peanut butter cup candies, cut in half, for the larger peanut butter cup candies, if desired.

Celebrate with Style

You can spend more time with Dad by preparing this dessert the day ahead. Serve with a carafe of freshly brewed coffee for the perfect ending to his special day.

All-American Celebration Cake

For a star-spangled finale, serve this easy berry-topped cake complete with sparkling candles.

Prep time: 25 minutes
Bake time: 35-40 minutes
Cool time: 1 hour
Chill time: 2 hours

1   package (16 ounces) angel food cake mix

1   lemon

1/2 cup powdered sugar

3   cups strawberries, sliced (12 ounces)

1/2 pint fresh blueberries (about 1 cup)

1/2 pint fresh raspberries (about 1 cup)

1   container (8 ounces) frozen whipped topping, thawed

Fresh mint leaves (optional)

1. Preheat oven to 350°F. Prepare cake mix according to package directions. Pour batter into ungreased **Rectangular Baker**, spreading evenly. Bake on center rack in oven 35-40 minutes or until top is golden brown and the cracks feel dry and not sticky. (Cake should be firm to the touch; do not underbake.) Carefully turn baker upside down onto **Cooling Rack**; cool completely. (Do not remove cake from baker.)

2. Zest whole lemon using **Lemon Zester/Scorer**. Juice lemon using **Juicer** to measure 2 tablespoons juice. Whisk lemon juice, zest and powdered sugar in **Classic Batter Bowl** until smooth.

3. Slice strawberries using **Egg Slicer Plus®**. Add strawberries, blueberries and raspberries to sugar mixture; mix gently with **Mix 'N Scraper®** to coat fruit.

4. Using **Nylon Fork** or large fork, poke holes in cake about 1 1/2 inches deep and 1/2 inch apart. Spoon fruit mixture over cake to within 1/2 inch of edges. Refrigerate at least 2 hours to allow juices to soak into cake.

5. Just before serving, attach closed star tip to **Easy Accent® Decorator**; fill with whipped topping and pipe evenly around edge of cake. To serve, cut into squares. Garnish each serving with additional whipped topping and mint leaves, if desired.

Yield: 15 servings

LOW FAT   Nutrients per serving: Calories 190, Total Fat 3 g, Saturated Fat 3 g, Cholesterol 0 mg, Carbohydrate 37 g, Protein 3 g, Sodium 220 mg, Fiber 1 g

Diabetic exchanges per serving: 1 starch, 1 1/2 fruit, 1/2 fat (2 1/2 carb)

Cook's Tips

This cake can be prepared up to 6 hours in advance.

*Use the **Serrated Bread Knife** to easily cut through the tender angel food cake.*

Celebrate with Style

For a summer menu that deserves a 4-star rating, start with *Honey Mustard Dip* (p. 39) served with pretzels and fresh vegetable dippers. Follow with *Grilled Italian Sausages with Confetti Vegetable Relish* (p. 79) accompanied by *Picnic Potato Salad* (p. 80). Then, get ready for the cheers when you bring out our spectacular *All-American Celebration Cake*.

Ultimate Banana Split Cake

Coated in caramel and adorned with chocolate, fruit and whipped topping, this cake is truly a work of art.

Prep time: 45 minutes
Bake time: 40-45 minutes
Cool time: 1 hour

Cake

- 1 package (18.25 ounces) yellow cake mix (plus ingredients to make cake)
- 1 package (3.4 ounces) banana cream instant pudding and pie filling

Toppings

- 1 tablespoon vegetable oil
- 2/3 cup peanuts, divided
- 1 cup butterscotch caramel ice cream topping
- 1/2 cup semi-sweet chocolate morsels, melted
- 1 banana, sliced
- 2 cups thawed, frozen whipped topping
- 1 can (8 ounces) pineapple slices, drained and patted dry
- 7 large whole strawberries
- Ice cream (optional)

1. Preheat oven to 350°F. Spray **Deep Dish Baker** with nonstick cooking spray. In **Classic Batter Bowl**, combine cake and pudding mixes. Prepare cake according to package directions. Pour batter into baker. Bake 40-45 minutes or until top 'of cake springs back when lightly pressed. Cool 10 minutes; invert onto **Cooling Rack** and remove baker. Cool completely.

2. Brush clean baker with vegetable oil. Chop 1/2 cup of the peanuts using **Food Chopper**. In **Small Batter Bowl**, combine peanuts and ice cream topping; pour into baker. Microwave on HIGH 1 1/2 minutes; tilt baker to coat bottom. Place cake, right side up, into baker. Press down around edge to allow caramel mixture to come up sides of cake. Carefully invert cake onto **Round Platter**. Scrape any remaining caramel mixture from baker onto cake.

3. In **Small Micro-Cooker®**, microwave chocolate morsels, uncovered, on HIGH 1-1 1/2 minutes, stirring after each 20-second interval or until melted. Pipe 12 flower-shaped decorations onto **Parchment Paper** (see Cook's Tips). Place 1 peanut in center of each flower; refrigerate 15 minutes. Slice banana into 12 slices; place evenly around top edge of cake. Drizzle remaining chocolate over banana slices.

4. Fill **Easy Accent® Decorator** with whipped topping; pipe rosettes slightly overlapping banana slices. Using **Deluxe Cheese Grater**, grate remaining peanuts over rosettes. Cut 3 pineapple slices into quarters; place between rosettes. Place 1 chocolate decoration on each rosette.

5. Slice 6 strawberries in half; place against side of cake. Garnish center of cake with remaining strawberry. Serve with ice cream, if desired.

Yield: 12 servings

Nutrients per serving: Calories 510, Total Fat 30 g, Saturated Fat 5 g, Cholesterol 55 mg, Carbohydrate 74 g, Protein 6 g, Sodium 500 mg, Fiber 2 g
Diabetic exchanges per serving: 2 starch, 3 fruit, 6 fat (5 carb)

Cook's Tips

*For chocolate garnishes, place a small, resealable plastic food storage bag inside the **Measure-All® Cup**. Pour melted chocolate into corner of bag. Twist top of bag; secure with **Twixit! Clip**. Cut a small tip off corner of bag to allow the chocolate to flow through.*

Create a five-petal flower by gently squeezing the chocolate in a circular pattern, starting and ending in the center.

*Use the **Egg Slicer Plus®** for easily slicing the banana and for creating a strawberry fan for center of cake.*

If preparing this recipe ahead, brush the banana slices with lemon juice to prevent them from turning brown. Pat dry before placing on the cake.

*To make cutting the cake easier, dip the **Utility Knife** into warm water.*

Cappuccino Mousse Trifle

This quick and easy trifle is cool, creamy and oh, so dreamy.

Prep time: 20 minutes
Chill time: 30 minutes

1   frozen prepared pound cake
    (16 ounces)
2 1/2   cups cold milk
1/3   cup instant coffee granules
2   packages (3.4 ounces each)
    vanilla instant pudding and
    pie filling
2   containers (8 ounces each) frozen
    whipped topping, thawed,
    divided
1   square (1 ounce) semi-sweet
    chocolate for baking
1/4   teaspoon Pantry Korintje
    Cinnamon

1. Cut pound cake into 1-inch cubes using **Serrated Bread Knife**; set aside.

2. In **Classic Batter Bowl**, whisk milk and instant coffee granules using **Stainless Steel Whisk**. Let stand 5 minutes or until dissolved.

3. Pour 1 cup of the milk mixture into **Measure-All® Cup**; set aside. Add pudding mixes to remaining milk mixture in batter bowl; whisk until mixture begins to thicken. Gently fold in one container of whipped topping using **Classic Scraper**.

4. To assemble trifle, place one third of the cake cubes in bottom of chilled **Chillzanne® Bowl**. Pour one third of the reserved milk mixture evenly over cake cubes. Top with one third of the pudding mixture, pressing lightly. Using **Deluxe Cheese Grater**, grate 1/4 of the chocolate over pudding mixture. Repeat layers 2 more times. Reserve the remaining chocolate for garnish.

5. Fill **Easy Accent® Decorator** with 1 cup of the remaining whipped topping; set aside. Using **Large Spreader**, spread remaining whipped topping over entire top of trifle, creating a smooth surface. Pipe rosettes around edge of dessert. Grate remaining chocolate in center; sprinkle lightly with cinnamon. For a colder serving temperature, refrigerate at least 30 minutes.

Yield: 10 servings

Nutrients per serving: Calories 440, Total Fat 20 g, Saturated Fat 15 g, Cholesterol 105 mg, Carbohydrate 57 g, Protein 5 g, Sodium 490 mg, Fiber less than 1 g
Diabetic exchanges per serving: 2 starch, 2 fruit, 4 fat (4 carb)

Cook's Tips

This trifle can be assembled several hours before serving, or even the night before.

For a lighter version, substitute skim milk for milk and thawed fat-free frozen whipped topping for the whipped topping.

Celebrate with Style

This trifle makes a lovely alternative to cake for adult birthday parties. For a personal touch, omit the grated chocolate on top of the trifle and write a birthday message with melted chocolate over the whipped topping. Don't forget the candles!

Ice Cream Pizza

Prep time: 30 minutes
Cook time: 10 minutes
Cool time: 10 minutes
Freeze time: 1 hour
 or overnight

*This make-ahead dessert sensation is perfect for a birthday or any summer celebration.
Ask the birthday celebrant to choose his or her favorite ice cream, fruit and toppings!*

1/2	cup light corn syrup
1/4	cup butter or margarine
1/4	cup packed brown sugar
6	cups crispy rice cereal
1	container (1/2 gallon) Neapolitan or vanilla ice cream
2	cups thawed, frozen whipped topping
1	cup sliced strawberries
	Chocolate-flavored syrup (optional)
	Colored sprinkles, decors, miniature chocolate morsels or chopped nuts (optional)

1. Cut a circle of **Parchment Paper** to fit bottom of **Chillzanne® Platter**; place parchment circle on platter.

2. Combine corn syrup, butter and brown sugar in **Professional (4-qt.) Casserole**. Cook over medium heat; stirring occasionally until mixture begins to boil. Remove from heat. Add cereal; stir until well coated. Press mixture evenly over bottom of platter. Cool completely.

3. Scoop ice cream into balls using **Large Scoop**; arrange over cooled crust. Cover with plastic wrap; freeze 1 hour or overnight. (Recipe can be made several days in advance up to this step.)

4. When ready to serve, attach open star tip to **Easy Accent® Decorator**; fill with whipped topping. Pipe whipped topping between scoops of ice cream. Garnish with strawberry slices. Drizzle chocolate syrup over pizza; top with candy decorations or nuts, if desired. Cut into wedges using **Nylon Knife**.

Yield: 16 servings

Nutrients per serving: Calories 260, Total Fat 12 g, Saturated Fat 8 g, Cholesterol 35 mg, Carbohydrate 38 g, Protein 3 g, Sodium 210 mg, Fiber 0 g
Diabetic exchanges per serving: 1 starch, 1 1/2 fruit, 2 fat (2 1/2 carb)

Cook's Tips

*Place the Chillzanne®
Platter in the freezer
4 hours or overnight prior
to making this recipe. The
platter has a unique food-
safe gel within the bottom
of the platter. Once frozen,
it will keep the dessert icy
cold while serving.*

*Blueberries, raspberries or
banana slices can be
substituted for the
strawberries.*

*The **Egg Slicer Plus®** is
great for quickly slicing
strawberries or bananas.*

*Use the Nylon Knife when
cutting on the platter so as
not to scratch the surface.*

Celebrate with Style

Instead of a birthday cake, why not surprise everyone with this colorful ice cream novelty?
For a special presentation, decorate with long, brightly burning tapers that will last
through the many hoped-for birthday wishes.

Very Cherry Ice

Nothing says summer like a refreshing, frozen treat. Shave the ice and serve in dessert cups or mix with soda for a frosty slush.

Prep time: 10 minutes
Freeze time: 8 hours
or overnight

2¼ cups water

⅓ cup sugar

1 large lemon

1 can (12 ounces) frozen apple-cherry or cherry drink concentrate

1. In **Small (2-qt.) Saucepan**, bring water and sugar to a boil over medium-high heat, stirring occasionally. Reduce heat; simmer 5 minutes. Remove from heat.

2. Juice lemon with **Juicer** to measure 3 tablespoons juice. Stir lemon juice and concentrate into sugar syrup. Divide mixture evenly among 3 **Ice Shaver Tubs**; freeze until firm.

3. Remove frozen mixture from tubs; shave using **Ice Shaver** into chilled **Chillzanne® Mini-Bowl**. Scoop into small cups.

Yield: 8 servings

LOW FAT Nutrients per serving: Calories 130, Total Fat 0 g, Saturated Fat 0 g, Cholesterol 0 mg, Carbohydrate 32 g, Protein 0 g, Sodium 15 mg, Fiber 0 g
Diabetic exchanges per serving: 2 fruit (2 carb)

Cook's Tips

To easily remove the frozen ice mixtures from the plastic tubs, line tubs with plastic wrap before filling.

Three cups chilled seltzer water can be substituted for the ginger ale, if desired.

Place the Chillzanne® Mini-Bowl in the freezer at the same time that you freeze the cherry mixture. It will keep the shaved ice frosty for serving and can be used to store any leftovers.

Very Cherry Slush

(Pictured on p. 123)

3 tubs frozen **Very Cherry Ice** (see above)

2 cans (12 ounces each) chilled ginger ale carbonated soda

1. Remove frozen mixture from tubs; shave using **Ice Shaver** into chilled **Chillzanne® Mini-Bowl**.

2. Place shaved ice and carbonated soda in **Quick-Stir® Pitcher**; plunge to mix. Pour into chilled glasses. Serve immediately.

Yield: 8 servings

LOW FAT Nutrients per serving (¾ cup): Calories 160, Total Fat 0 g, Saturated Fat 0 g, Cholesterol 0 mg, Carbohydrate 30 g, Protein 0 g, Sodium 20 mg, Fiber 0 g
Diabetic exchanges per serving: 2 fruit (2 carb)

Index

All-American Celebration Cake, 116

Appetizers
(see also Dips and Spreads)

Asian Sweet and Sour Meatballs, 9
Baked Brie with Apples
    & Cranberries, 6
Baked Brie with Pesto & Mushrooms, 6
Baked Pita Chips, 12
Barbecued Chicken Drumsticks, 32
Barbecue Snack Mix, 37
Canapé French Bread, 25
Chicken Enchilada Ring, 26
Fall Pizza, 19
Family-Style Calzone, 29
Fancy Deviled Eggs, 22
Four Seasons Appetizer Pizza, 19
Party Ham Puffs, 20
Party Salmon Puffs, 20
Plantain Chips, 34
Roast Beef Roll-Ups, 23
Shrimp Wonton Cups, 7
Southwestern Snack Squares, 31
Spring Pizza, 19
Stuffed Portobello Mushrooms, 15
Summer Pizza, 19
Turkey Roll-Ups, 23
Warm Olive Bruschetta, 16
Winter Pizza, 19

Apples

Baked Brie with Apples
    & Cranberries, 6
French Apple Pastry, 92
Harvest Honey Cake, 91
Step-Ahead Sweet Potato Bake, 51
Asian Sweet and Sour Meatballs, 9
Bacon, Lettuce & Tomato Dip, 25
Baked Brie with Apples & Cranberries, 6
Baked Brie with Pesto & Mushrooms, 6
Baked Pita Chips, 12
Barbecued Chicken Drumsticks, 32
Barbecue Snack Mix, 37

Beans

Mexican Two Bean Chicken Chili, 68
Southern-Style Salsa, 35
Southwestern Snack Squares, 31

Beef

Asian Sweet and Sour Meatballs, 9
Herb Seasoned Beef Rib Roast, 42
Individual Beef Wellingtons, 57
Party Pasta Bowl, 67
Roast Beef Roll-Ups, 23
Savory Beef Brisket, 47
Southwestern Snack Squares, 31
Birthday Blastoff Cake, 113

Breads

Baked Pita Chips, 12
Canapé French Bread, 25
Candy Cane Coffee Cake, 98
Cherry Eggnog Tea Bread, 97
Family-Style Calzone, 29
Individual Yorkshire Puddings, 43
Bride-to-Be Party Cake, 112

Cakes

All-American Celebration Cake, 116
Blastoff Birthday Cake, 113
Bride-to-Be Party Cake, 112
Harvest Honey Cake, 91
Ultimate Banana Split Cake, 119
Calypso Peach Salsa, 34
Canapé French Bread, 25
Candy Cane Coffee Cake, 98
Cappuccino Mousse Trifle, 120
Cheesecake Tartlets, 112
Cherry Eggnog Tea Bread, 97
Chicken Enchilada Ring, 26
Chicken Lasagna Alfredo, 70
Chicken Pesto Sandwich Ring, 82

Chocolate

Chocolate Caramel Oatmeal Chews, 107
Chocolate Cookies, 86
Chocolate Kiss Cookies, 89
Chocolate Tartlets, 112
Coconut Almond Brownie Squares, 102
Melted Chocolate, 88

Peanut Butter Rocky Road Dessert, 114
Tuxedo Brownie Cups, 100
Coconut Almond Brownie Squares, 102

Cookies and Bars

All-Occasion Cookies, 86
Chocolate Caramel Oatmeal Chews, 107
Chocolate Cookies, 86
Chocolate Kiss Cookies, 89
Coconut Almond Brownie Squares, 102
Cutout Cookie Sandwiches, 89
Decorator Icing, 88
Melted Chocolate, 88
Peanut Butter Cookies, 86
Spice Cookies, 86
Thumbprint Cookies, 89
Tuxedo Brownie Cups, 100
Creamy Lemon Supreme, 109
Cutout Cookie Sandwiches, 89
Dazzle Berry Pie, 105
Decorator Icing, 88

Desserts (see also Cakes; Pies and Pastries)

Cappuccino Mousse Trifle, 120
Creamy Lemon Supreme, 109
Frosty Pumpkin Dessert, 94
Ice Cream Pizza, 122
Peanut Butter Rocky Road Dessert, 114
Very Cherry Ice, 124
Very Cherry Slush, 124

Dips and Spreads

Bacon, Lettuce & Tomato Dip, 25
Calypso Peach Salsa, 34
Honey Mustard Dip, 39
Hot Artichoke Crabmeat Dip, 12
Layered Athenian Cheese Spread, 10
Southern-Style Salsa, 35
Warm Olive Bruschetta, 16

Eggs

Fancy Deviled Eggs, 22
Sunrise Oven Omelet, 72
Fall Pizza, 19
Family-Style Calzone, 29
Fancy Deviled Eggs, 22
Festive Scalloped Corn, 61

Fish and Seafood

Hot Artichoke Crabmeat Dip, 12
Lemon-Dill Grilled Salmon &
　Asparagus, 75
Party Salmon Puffs, 20
Seafood Chowder, 55
Shrimp Wonton Cups, 7
Winter Pizza, 19
Four Seasons Appetizer Pizza, 19
French Apple Pastry, 92
Frosty Pumpkin Dessert, 94

Fruit (see also Apples)

All-American Celebration Cake, 116
Calypso Peach Salsa, 34
Candy Cane Coffee Cake, 98
Dazzle Berry Pie, 105
Ultimate Banana Split Cake, 119
Giant Potato Pancake, 49

Grilling

Chicken Pesto Sandwich Ring, 82
Grilled Asian Pork Tenderloin Salad, 76
Grilled Italian Sausages with Confetti
　Vegetable Relish, 79
Lemon-Dill Grilled Salmon &
　Asparagus, 75
Ham Florentine Wreath, 62
Harvest Honey Cake, 91
Herb Seasoned Beef Rib Roast, 42
Honey Mustard Dip, 39
Hot Artichoke Crabmeat Dip, 12
Hot Barbecued Chicken Drumsticks, 32
Ice Cream Pizza, 122
Individual Beef Wellingtons, 57
Individual Yorkshire Puddings, 43
Layered Athenian Cheese Spread, 10

Lemon

Creamy Lemon Supreme, 109
Lemon-Dill Grilled Salmon &
　Asparagus, 75
Lemony Chicken Popover Puff, 65
Teatime Tartlets, 111
Lemony Chicken Popover Puff, 65

Low Fat

All-American Celebration Cake, 116
Baked Pita Chips, 12
Calypso Peach Salsa, 34
Canapé French Bread, 25
Individual Yorkshire Puddings, 43
Mushroom Sauce, 43
Shrimp Wonton Cups, 7
Twice-Baked Potato Cups, 52
Very Cherry Ice, 124
Very Cherry Slush, 124
Melted Chocolate, 88
Mexican Two Bean Chicken Chili, 68

Mushrooms

Baked Brie with Pesto & Mushrooms, 6
Mushroom Sauce, 43
Stuffed Portobello Mushrooms, 15
Party Ham Puffs, 20
Party Pasta Bowl, 67
Party Salmon Puffs, 20

Pasta

Chicken Lasagna Alfredo, 70
Party Pasta Bowl, 67
Peanut Butter Cookies, 86
Peanut Butter Rocky Road Dessert, 114
Picnic Potato Salad, 80

Pies and Pastries

Candy Cane Coffee Cake, 98
Cheesecake Tartlets, 112
Chocolate Tartlets, 112
Dazzle Berry Pie, 105
French Apple Pastry, 92
Teatime Tartlets, 111

Pork

Bacon, Lettuce & Tomato Dip, 25
Family-Style Calzone, 29
Grilled Asian Pork Tenderloin Salad, 76
Grilled Italian Sausages with Confetti
　Vegetable Relish, 79
Ham Florentine Wreath, 62
Party Ham Puffs, 20
Spring Pizza, 19
Tangy Mustard Glazed Ham, 58

Potatoes

Giant Potato Pancake, 49
Picnic Potato Salad, 80
Step-Ahead Sweet Potato Bake, 51
Twice-Baked Potato Cups, 52

Poultry

Asian Sweet and Sour Meatballs, 9
Barbecued Chicken Drumsticks, 32
Chicken Enchilada Ring, 26
Chicken Lasagna Alfredo, 70
Chicken Pesto Sandwich Ring, 82
Lemony Chicken Popover Puff, 65
Hot Barbecued Chicken Drumsticks, 32
Mexican Two Bean Chicken Chili, 68
Roast Breast of Turkey with Apple
　Scented Pan Gravy, 44
Turkey Roll-Ups, 23
Roast Beef Roll-Ups, 23
Roast Breast of Turkey with Apple
　Scented Pan Gravy, 44
Roasted Spring Vegetables, 46
Roasted Winter Vegetables, 46

Sandwiches

Chicken Pesto Sandwich Ring, 82
Grilled Italian Sausages with Confetti
　Vegetable Relish, 79
Roast Beef Roll-Ups, 23
Turkey Roll-Ups, 23
Savory Beef Brisket, 47

Seafood (see Fish and Seafood)

Seafood Chowder, 55
Shrimp Wonton Cups, 7

Soups

Mexican Two Bean Chicken Chili, 68
Seafood Chowder, 55
Southern-Style Salsa, 35
Southwestern Snack Squares, 31
Spice Cookies, 86

Spinach

Chicken Lasagna Alfredo, 70
Chicken Pesto Sandwich Ring, 82
Ham Florentine Wreath, 62
Layered Athenian Cheese Spread, 10

pring Pizza, 19
ep-Ahead Sweet Potato Bake, 51
uffed Portobello Mushrooms, 15
ummer Pizza, 19
unrise Oven Omelet, 72
angy Mustard Glazed Ham, 58
eatime Tartlets, 111
humbprint Cookies, 89
urkey Roll-Ups, 23
uxedo Brownie Cups, 100
wice-Baked Potato Cups, 52
ltimate Banana Split Cake, 119

egetables (see also Potatoes)

Festive Scalloped Corn, 61
Lemon-Dill Grilled Salmon &
    Asparagus, 75
Plantain Chips, 34
Roasted Spring Vegetables, 46
Roasted Winter Vegetables, 46
ery Cherry Ice, 124
ery Cherry Slush, 124
Varm Olive Bruschetta, 16
Vinter Pizza, 19

toneware Index

Baking Bowl

Party Pasta Bowl, 67
Tangy Mustard Glazed Ham*, 58

Bar Pan

Barbecued Chicken Drumsticks, 32
Coconut Almond Brownie Squares, 102
Individual Beef Wellingtons, 57
Roasted Summer Vegetables, 46
Roasted Winter Vegetables, 46
Southwestern Snack Squares, 31

Deep Dish Baker

Asian Sweet and Sour Meatballs, 9
Hot Artichoke Crabmeat Dip, 12
Lemony Chicken Popover Puff, 65
Roast Breast of Turkey with Apple
    Scented Pan Gravy, 44
Stuffed Portobello Mushrooms, 15

Tangy Mustard Glazed Ham*, 58
Twice-Baked Potato Cups, 52
Ultimate Banana Split Cake, 119

Deep Dish Pie Plate

Dazzle Berry Pie, 105
Sunrise Oven Omelet, 72

Flat Baking Stone, Any (see also Rectangle Stone; Round Stones)

All-Occasion Cookies, 86
Baked Pita Chips, 12
Canapé French Bread, 25
Chocolate Cookies, 86
Chocolate Kiss Cookies, 89
Cutout Cookie Sandwiches, 89
Peanut Butter Cookies, 86
Spice Cookies, 86
Thumbprint Cookies, 89
Tinted Cookies, 87

Fluted Pan

Harvest Honey Cake, 91

Loaf Pan

Cherry Eggnog Tea Bread, 97

Muffin Pan

Cheesecake Tartlets, 112
Chocolate Tartlets, 112
Individual Yorkshire Puddings, 43
Teatime Tartlets, 111
Twice-Baked Potato Cups, 52

Oval Carving Platter Set/Oval Platter

Barbecued Chicken Drumsticks, 32
Herb Seasoned Beef Rib Roast, 42
Roast Breast of Turkey with Apple
    Scented Pan Gravy, 44
Tangy Mustard Glazed Ham, 58

Oval Baker

Festive Scalloped Corn, 61

Rectangle Stone

Candy Cane Coffee Cake, 98
Fall Pizza, 19
Four Seasons Appetizer Pizza, 19

Party Ham Puffs, 20
Party Salmon Puffs, 20
Spring Pizza, 19
Summer Pizza, 19
Winter Pizza, 19

Rectangular Baker

All-American Celebration Cake, 116
Barbecue Snack Mix, 37
Chicken Lasagna Alfredo, 70
Chocolate Caramel Oatmeal Chews, 107
Family-Style Calzone, 29
Herb Seasoned Beef Rib Roast, 42
Savory Beef Brisket, 47

Round Platter

Ham Florentine Wreath, 62
Ultimate Banana Split Cake, 119
Warm Olive Bruschetta, 16

Round Stones

Chicken Enchilada Ring, 26
Chicken Pesto Sandwich Ring, 82
Fall Pizza, 19
Four Seasons Appetizer Pizza, 19
French Apple Pastry, 92
Ham Florentine Wreath, 62
Spring Pizza, 19
Summer Pizza, 19
Warm Olive Bruschetta, 16
Winter Pizza, 19

Small Bar Pan

Baked Brie with Apples & Cranberries, 6
Baked Brie with Pesto & Mushrooms, 6
Individual Beef Wellingtons, 57

Square Baker

Peanut Butter Rocky Road Dessert, 114
Step-Ahead Sweet Potato Bake, 51

*Recipe uses two stoneware pieces in combination during cooking.

About Our Recipes

All recipes were developed and tested in The Pampered Chef Test Kitchens by professional home economists. For best results, we recommend you use the ingredients indicated in the recipe. The preparation and cooking times at the beginning of each recipe serve as a helpful guide when planning your time in the kitchen. As an important first step, we suggest you read through the recipe and assemble the necessary ingredients and equipment. "Prep time" is the approximate amount of time needed to prepare recipe ingredients before a final "Cook time." Prep time includes active steps such as chopping and mixing. It can also include cooking ingredients for a recipe that is assembled and then baked. Some preparation steps can be done simultaneously or during cooking and are usually indicated by the term "meanwhile." Some recipes that have steps not easily separated have a combined "Prep and cook time."

Notes on Nutrition

The nutrition information in *Celebrate! Family, Friends & Great Food* can help you decide how specific recipes can fit into your overall meal plan. At the end of each recipe, we list calories, total fat, saturated fat, cholesterol, carbohydrate, protein, sodium, and fiber. We also include diabetic exchange information commonly used by people with diabetes. This information is based on the 1995 *Exchange Lists for Meal Planning* by the American Diabetes Association and the American Dietetic Association. For each recipe, two lists of exchanges are provided. The first option is based on the traditional method of figuring diabetic exchanges; the second option is given in parentheses and reflects the newer system of carbohydrate counting. If you use the exchanges, consult your doctor, certified diabetes educator or registered dietitian.

Nutritional analysis for each recipe is based on the first ingredient listed whenever a choice is given and does not include optional ingredients, garnishes, fat used to grease pans, or serving suggestions. The ingredients used in our recipes and for nutritional analyses are based on most commonly purchased foods and unless indicated otherwise use 2 percent reduced-fat milk and large eggs. Recipes requiring ground beef are analyzed based on 90 percent lean ground beef. Recipes requiring ground turkey are analyzed based on 93 percent lean ground turkey. When margarine is an ingredient option, use a product containing 80 percent fat and not vegetable oil spread. Recipes labeled as LOW FAT have 3 grams or less fat per serving.

Metric Conversion Chart

Volume Measurements (dry)	Volume Measurements (fluid)	Dimensions
⅛ teaspoon = 0.6 mL	1 fluid ounce (2 tablespoons) = 30 mL	⅛ inch = 3 mm
¼ teaspoon = 1.25 mL	4 fluid ounces (½ cup) = 125 mL	¼ inch = 6 mm
½ teaspoon = 2.5 mL	8 fluid ounces (1 cup) = 250 mL	½ inch = 1 cm
¾ teaspoon = 3.75 mL	12 fluid ounces (1½ cups) = 375 mL	¾ inch = 2 cm
1 teaspoon = 5 mL	16 fluid ounces (2 cups) = 500 mL	1 inch = 2.5 cm
1 tablespoon = 15 mL		
2 tablespoons = 30 mL	**Weights (mass)**	**Oven Temperatures**
¼ cup = 50 mL		250°F = 120°C
⅓ cup = 75 mL	1 ounce = 30 g	275°F = 140°C
½ cup = 125 mL	4 ounces = 125 g	300°F = 150°C
⅔ cup = 150 mL	8 ounces = 250 g	325°F = 160°C
¾ cup = 175 mL	12 ounces = 350 g	350°F = 180°C
1 cup = 250 mL	16 ounces = 1 pound = 500 g	375°F = 190°C
		400°F = 200°C
		425°F = 220°C
Recipes in this cookbook have not been tested using metric measures. When converting and preparing recipes with metric measures, some variations in quality may be noticed.		450°F = 230°C